150 THEMES IN ART

Hans Meyers

B. T. BATSFORD LTD LONDON

© Otto Maier Verlag, Ravensburg, 1964

First English Language Edition, 1965

MADE AND PRINTED IN DENMARK
BY F. E. BORDING LTD, COPENHAGEN AND LONDON
FOR THE PUBLISHERS
B. T. BATSFORD LTD
4 FITZHARDINGE STREET, LONDON, W. 1

The pictorial themes of childhood and adolescence are inspired by the very different realms of reality and fantasy and, as a medium of art education, offer varied scope to the teacher.

The two realms of experience are here mapped out in 150 examples which become the framework of a comprehensive programme of art education and of actual teaching practice. Technical and psychological problems are encountered in each lesson, not merely theoretically but as a practical method. It will be seen from the ages of the pupils that nearly all the subjects can be tackled step by step at various ages and stages of development. It is essential that the teacher should adapt the sequence of tasks to the developmental needs of pupils and class. Although this keeping in step is above all a matter of sympathetic understanding, it is nevertheless helpful to bear in mind that the two main thematic cycles should recur at suitable intervals and should not be mutually exclusive.

Contents

3A1 *Winter Sport Mnd. Scene – Tones A lest.*

OCCUPATION

TECHNICAL ENVIRONMENT

TRAFFIC

C *The Natural and Architectural Environment*

STILL LIFE

PLANTS

ANIMALS

ARCHITECTURE

ALLEGORY AND PARABLE

ADVENTURE AND BALLAD

EXOTIC ADVENTURE

F *Themes of Fantasy and Utopian Dream*

FABULOUS BEINGS

FABULOUS BEASTS

WONDROUS AND FANTASTIC OBJECTS

THE WORLD OF MYSTERY AND ENCHANTMENT

THE SINISTER AND UNCANNY

9

The Illustrations

13

The cover design, Fantastic Birds, in paper batik, is by a student teacher

I THEMES FROM VISUAL IMAGES

A THE WORLD OF IMMEDIATE EXPERIENCE

THE FAMILY

Self-portrait (all ages)   A 1

> Painting in poster colours on drawing block (also in powder colours
> on 'kitchen' or shelf paper). Bristle brushes; if necessary, charcoal
> or pencils. (Also underglass painting with poster paints.)

The self-portrait is one of the numerous subjects which promise
success at every age. It offers ever new opportunities for self-
expression and interpretation as well to the three-year-old as
to the mature artist in his old age. It should recur at judicious
intervals throughout school life. A change of medium brings
renewed interest.

Method

The older the child, the more importance should be attached
to composition. Here is an opportunity for large-scale work.
Half-length, head and shoulders, or head only offer the advantage
of concentration on the essentials and of a simple plan of composition, while a full-length figure easily leads to empty expanses
on each side of the figure and is more to be recommended for
young children for whom a conscious limitation of the subject
would be unnatural. Full-face should be preferred to profile
since one normally sees, and therefore pictures, oneself full-face
(Colour Plate I).

If the pupils are not to paint immediately—though they
might well be allowed to do so—a drawing in pencil (or charcoal if the block is large) may form the basis of the painting.
The carrying out of the drawing, the order of the detail, the
decision as to whether the outline of the face or the features
be drawn first, will be left to the pupil. This does not preclude
some preparatory hints (from 8 upwards) on the proportions
and placing of the drawing in relation to the given area of the
paper. Subsequent help may be given, if need be (in the form
of verbal hints, but not by direct drawing in), without violating
the child's own sense of achievement. Fuzziness of line in
drawing, technical difficulties in painting or in the disposition

15

of masses and gross mistakes of proportion (from 10 upwards), these are the most essential occasions for giving simple hints. Even the colouring plan should be influenced beforehand only in general, not in detail—colour to be applied in a broad wash; detailed brush strokes to be applied if necessary on top of the original ground colour of the face, to emphasise the nose, mouth, etc.; gradations of colour possibly to be painted in working wet into wet, or to be applied afterwards. A harmoniously keyed colour for the background heightens the effect of the picture as a colour composition. Here too a thick textured colour with plenty of pigment is the best means of achieving a vivid and expressive result.

A 2   **Family portrait (all ages)**

> Opaque colour. Poster colours, drawing block, pencil and brush (also powder colours, with bristle brush, on large sheets of 'kitchen' paper).

The great attraction of this subject is that it contains no detail in which the artist is not intimately involved. The self-portrait already demanded that he should represent himself vividly and objectively for the public view. With his mother and father, brother and sister, it is also to some extent a matter of 'exposure' not only of them, but of his own personal relationship with them. This task is a more taxing one for the higher age groups, touching deep feelings and inhibitions. At the same time it is very useful, as it leads to a confrontation of the intimate sphere with the outside world; experience has shown that this confrontation involves an attempt to express qualitative values and so raises self-consciousness to a plane where it may be neutralised and overcome.

Method

The younger child composes his family portrait as a decorative row of figures, in the style of ancient family photographs, which has an old-world charm to our modern eyes. Older children are more interested in presenting some lively scene from family life, a walk in the woods or an evening round the fireside. We can allow such interest full scope, while demanding that care be given to the portrayal of the main figures and objects in the picture and to the detail necessary for its completion.

16

Plate 1

Mother at the Mirror (A3), in poster colours, by an 11-year-old girl. Height 22 inches

Plate 2

b Me and my Scooter (A7),
in powder colours, by a 12-
year-old boy. Height 40 inches

c Ball Game (A8), in poster
colours, by a 13-year-old girl.
Height 18 inches

d Roller-skaters (A9),
cut, by a 15-year-old
Height 19 inches

Good likenesses in the photographic sense must not be expected. In the art of infants and young children, likeness does not exist but is a matter of attributes, of characteristic features. The father wears a hat or a beard, a collar and tie, and big sister her glasses or necklace. Basically however, a good likeness depends upon the involvement of the artist himself in his portrait, since his own inner character inevitably penetrates the inner character of his subject. This intuitive inner likeness is even, in a sense, superior to outward resemblance.

Direct painting will heighten the expressive power of the picture, while careful planning of the composition and detailed drawing will increase its individuality. Either treatment is valid, but neither must be used exclusively if we would avoid on the one hand undisciplined formlessness, on the other pedantic fussiness.

Mother at the Mirror (all ages) A 3

> Thick paint, possibly over pencil sketch. Drawing block, large if possible; box of poster colours and sable brush.

The two attributes required of any subject are that it should be suitable for a child and suitable for a picture; the first requirement must receive first consideration in the junior school, the second in the upper school. The present subject fills these requirements well since both the idea and its formal realisation are pictorially stimulating.

Method

The mother stands in front of the mirror. Her characteristic gestures in putting on her hat or making up, her appraising glances at her reflection can be brought to mind by lively mimicry best done by the children themselves, perhaps in the form of a charade. Imagined as a picture, the subject is especially fascinating (Plate 1). The length of the paper is best used vertically. The mother is represented twice, either back and front view, or as two profiles turned towards one another (by the younger children, of course, in all kinds of symbolic representation which cannot be judged by visual standards). Her reflected gestures produce a play of rhythm. How the closer linking of figure with reflection achieves a stronger compositional unity will be discussed with older pupils. The importance of the size of the figures in proportion to the whole picture should also be understood from the start; the more the subject fills the picture area, the better. Subjects like this, which are limited to a few large figures, or objects, assist concentration (particularly of ten-year-olds and upwards), which is dependent upon conscientious absorbtion in the task. As regards colour composition, such subjects adapt themselves to a complete painting of the picture area. In subjects with numerous small figures, the background is better left plain, especially by younger children. A thick application of paint with plenty of pigment heightens the sensuous appeal of the picture.

Further themes: Cleaning my Teeth; Helping Mother Hang out the Washing; Dinnertime; Daddy Shaving; Grandma Knitting; Pushing the Pram (Baby Carriage); My Dream; Self-Portrait with Musical Instrument; A Family Visit; Music at Home.

SCHOOL

A 4   **In the School Corridor (10-14)**

> Preliminary pencil sketch on painting paper; painting with thick colour. HB pencil, drawing block 24×18 inches; box of poster colours and brush No. 3 or 6; or equivalent materials.

My aim is to give girls, who have just entered secondary school and a new class and community, an unforgettable experience of the art class. This moment is a particularly promising and fruitful one; no age group is more co-operative or enthusiastic. What a delightful surprise it is when the large drawing blocks (24 ×18 inches) are brought out! The school is run by Ursuline nuns whose religious habit, gentle manner and care of their new pupils make a deep impression. The school corridor is the scene of many of the children's meetings with the nuns. It is also a picture gallery, where the paintings of the seniors are exhibited. So I have discovered a theme for a picture that will be a surprise, not only to the rest of the school, but above all to the Sisters themselves, and that also possesses an aura of secrecy—'Conversation with the Sisters in the School Corridor' (Plate 2 a).

20

Method

It was five weeks before we were ready to make our 'coup' and hang 16 pictures outside in the corridor all at once. The surprise effect was completely successful: children from the other classes and the Sisters crowded round the pictures like a swarm of bees. The junior class had made its debut and each member had contributed to the work. The length of the picture space, used horizontally, was sufficient for several figures, their number determined by the subject itself and by the demands of compositional completeness (no 'empty spaces'). The background could be filled by the classroom door, the peg-racks and the pictures in the slide-in frames. Anyone who liked could paint a miniature version of a 'School Corridor' picture into one of the frames, even a miniature replica of her own picture. There was much surreptitious study of the Sisters' habit throughout the task and the pious ladies were subjected to a lot of physiognomic comparison. Before painting was begun, a careful drawing was demanded of each pupil. The painting presented scarcely any technical difficulties. A few brief hints were sufficient: on holding the brush (in an upright position, the tip pointed from inwards towards the outline of the area to be painted to avoid 'going over the edge') and on concentrating entirely on some single detail at the start.

A Team at the Parallel Bars (10 upwards)   A 5

> Painted pencil drawing on a neutral background. Drawing block, pencil, box of poster colours, brush.

School life not only offers occasions for works of art as school decoration (posters, notices, etc., as well as exhibitions), but is itself an inexhaustible subject of art. What an endless series of events take place every day from the journey to school to the rush out of school, from choral singing to climbing practice in the gym. But all this, if it is to be represented pictorially, must first be thought of as a picture. This is the chief task of the art teacher as well as of the pupil. From ten years of age upwards, the conscious representation of form begins gradually to take the place of the younger child's spontaneous expression of his experience. The subject 'A Team at the Parallel Bars' is chosen so that a ten-year-old can master the simple intersections between the gymnastic equipment and the team of

21

children in the gymnasium, and, in so doing, construct a clear picture. This type of subject is chosen in order to evoke directly a complete and self-explanatory picture.

Method

The experience to be represented holds nothing unfamiliar to the pupil. Nevertheless a special repetition of the situation in the form of a physical re-enactment is rewarding in this as in many similar subjects. If pupils are led to consider an already familiar scene, knowing that they are to paint or draw it, conscious observation will modify their mental image in individual directions. This process of observation is essential, though a child obviously cannot make such intensive use of it as could a mature artist. This is the process of transformation by artistic vision which frees external reality of its inessential aspects. Forms lose their arbitrary and unrelated confusion, and their relationships of balance and movement become discernible. The inessential drops away; the essential remains. This essential is visual harmony, a visible rhythmic pattern.

For this reason, the pictorial visualisation of objects is important from ten years of age upwards. The more child-like the experience, the better. We experience the forms of the parallel bars for our picture. We consider various suggestions as to the disposition of the figures of the team in the picture. We imagine the way a boy swinging on the bars will appear in our picture. We exchange ideas about the colours of his clothes for our picture. The more often this experience occurs, the richer the visual experience of the child will become. Education in the art of seeing is education for life.

A 6   **Portrait of the Class (8 upwards)**

> Poster colour painting: group work, combination of separate contributions. Pencil, box of poster colours, brush, drawing block or loose sheets of painting paper, large background sheet of packing paper, paste or glue.

Many drops make an ocean. If every pupil in a class contributes, large decorative paintings can be produced in a short time. What an individual could never have achieved is easily achieved by the group. Group planning produces a realisable pictorial idea. Various possibilities are considered. Is it to be a picture of the class, with the teacher standing in front (one

22

pupil sees a picture with the teacher's back in the foreground) and the pupils sitting in their places (each pupil draws himself sitting at his desk in full-face)? Or is it to be a 'portrait' of the class in which each pupil portrays himself standing in full-length and cuts his figure out so that all can be pasted on to one big picture?

Method

We decide in favour of the second method. The average size of each figure is agreed upon and marked out on our blocks or sheets. For ten-year-olds, occasional hints on anatomical proportions may be useful: e.g., proportion of head to length of figure, arms reaching middle of thigh, beginning at shoulder-level, hands, usually drawn too small, are the same length as the face, the forehead the same length as the nose. More detailed observations follow from about 12 years upwards: asymmetrical almond-like formation of the eyes, the iris slightly covered by the upper lid, movement of the mouth and curvature of the lips, simple basic forms and movements of the hand.

When the drawing and painting of the full-length self-portrait is finished, everyone cuts out his figure carefully. All the completed cut-outs are then placed on the large sheet of packing paper for attempts at composite arrengement. The dull colour of packing paper makes an unsatisfactory background. An even coat of powder paint (made fast with size), particularly of a dark colour such as blue-black or dark green, applied to the background will heighten the final effect.

Composition practice with movable picture elements is a wonderful help in the teaching of composition and should be used to the full. Children's compositions are usually without any overlapping. Our subject lends itself to lively grouping of overlapping figures. When the most effective arrangement has been found, we mark the positions of the figures by signs or numbers and paste them on carefully.

Further themes: Our Teacher; Rope-climbing; A Class Excursion; On the School Staircase; The Ten O'Clock Break; Going to School; The School Choir; Dinner at School; My School Things; Helping with Housework.

A 7 **Me and my Scooter (6-12)**

> Painting either with powder colours and a bristle brush on 'scrap'
> paper, or with poster colours on a drawing block. Scissors and pins
> for cutting out and pinning to the wall for the group work, 'A
> Chain of Roller-Skaters'.

We should visualise the result of every art exercise. In this one,
our aim is as follows: a large classroom or hall wall is to be
decorated. We visualise the wall covered with many large cut-
outs forming a colourful chain of happy figures on scooters or
roller-skates, the girls coming from the right, the boys from the
left. Pins inserted unobtrusively at essential points hold the
whole mural decoration together. Scrap paper for painting is
the cheapest. Powder colours (red, green, yellow, blue, black),
mixed with gum arabic or some patent base, are prepared in
large jam-jars. To avoid muddy colours or constant brush-
washing, a few bristle brushes are allotted to each jar of colour.

Method

One boy and one girl demonstrate the movements of roller-
skating (preferably with skates on), hands on the rail, one leg
supporting, the other swung out. The large sheets of paper lie
on the tables, on the floor, or hang on the black-board. We
start with a brush drawing. Each pupil chooses one colour only
(not yellow) with which the outline and main lines of the figure
are brush-drawn. In order to avoid ineradicable mistakes and
waste of paper and to ensure the correct placing and size of the
various details, a few dots can be put in before drawing begins,
to show the position of wheels, guide-rail, top of the head, hips.
Pupils quite unpractised in drawing can if necessary make an
initial charcoal drawing which can be finalised with the brush.
Despite the simple monumental character of the painting, we
pay attention to careful rendering of features in profile and of
hands. The effect of the whole depends upon the quality of the
detail, which, if high will inevitably raise the quality of the rest
of the production (Plate 2b).

When the brush drawing is finished, the inner areas must be
painted in different colours. The choice of colour is, of course,
left free and is nearly always happy, since children have a sure
instinct. When the painting has dried and been cut out, the

composition arrangement for the mural begins. This can be tried out on the floor. A frieze arrangement or a grouping—loose or close—of figures, possibly overlapping, are alternatives.

Ball Game (10-18) A 8

> Pencil drawing followed by painting with poster colours. Drawing block, medium hard pencil, box of poster colours and brush.

Bat and ball games are among the favourite pastimes of the middle classes. As an art motif they can be treated in various ways: possibly in a group work for which the class is divided into two sides playing against each other, every player portraying himself; perhaps as an individual task which each one tackles in his own way.

Not every absorbing experience is a fertile pictorial subject: observation of the life-cycle of the frog, for example, is highly interesting to children, but offers no stimulus to artistic production. However life does provide innumerable outstandingly good themes like the present one. The teacher trained to picture awareness soon recognises the promising themes (such as Workman with a Concrete-Mixer; Cockfight; Hercules' Combat with the Lion) and can distinguish them from artificial themes (e.g. Hunting for Colorado Beetles; Napoleon returning from Exile; A Coral Reef).

Method

A ball game is experienced as a drama in which the player takes part. As he draws, a keen player is inspired by his memory to a vivid representation of bodies in movement. Pupils with a gift for drawing are often led on by such a dramatic subject to the most fantastic and diverse invention, giving the players exaggerated and striking attitudes. Such virtuosity is not necessarily of artistic value. It is easy to show them by positive examples that rhythmic repetition of similar pictorial elements produces a more artistically effective picture than mere arbitrary inventiveness (Plate 2 c). Pupils of average talent often have the least trouble in learning this lesson.

Children tire of a pictorial composition with many figures unless the task is divided into short-term objectives. For instance, the teacher can first concentrate their attention on the two leading players. When this task is completed and the teacher has confirmed its success, each succeeding stage successfully reached brings fresh encouragement and creative zest. The aim of this guidance by the teacher from one stage to another is to train the child to direct and concentrate his own powers. Thus the guiding reins, at first firmly held, may be gradually slackened in response to, and as a proof of confidence in, the child's increasing control of his own creative powers.

A 9 Roller-skaters (12 upwards)

Large lino cut. Any kind of paper for the first sketch; pencil, piece of plain lino of the softer kind, 10×14 inches, or cork lino; cutting tool; absorbent printing paper, small pane of glass, old newspapers; printing colour: an oil-based printing colour, soluble in turpentine.

Free artistic creation through the media of paint and drawing should be alternated with more disciplined creative work in techniques using more resistent media.

Each pupil should possess his own drawing block and paintbox for the art class. Other techniques require materials that must be provided. Linoleum-fitting firms will gladly supply remainders. The technique of lino-cutting and printing is described in technical works (see *150 Techniques in Art*, p. 57*). Subjects with large figures are the most suitable for this technique.

Method

On pieces of scrap paper several sketches are made to compose the two figures into a well unified picture. Pupils must know already that these two figures are to fill a picture space of the height and breadth of the lino plate. The most successful design is redrawn in pencil on the lino (Plate 2 d). (Beginners are given a sheet of paper the exact size of the lino). Transference to the lino need not be a mechanical process. Visual accuracy should rather be developed and a much livelier line will result. The cutting is most successfully done after the drawn lines have been scored with a penknife. The print of a single-line cut produces a white-line print on a black (or coloured) ground. From now on, it is possible, by cutting away the background of the picture round the figures, to produce a flat printing surface. Only the figures with their white inner lines are printed. This

---

* H. Meyers, *150 Techniques in Art*, 1963

lino-cut method with dark figures on a light ground is the surest way for the beginner to obtain a clear print.

In the white-figure cut the process is reversed. From the point of view of difficulty, it is the next stage in the art of lino cutting. These two methods showing the relationship of figures to background in its simplest form, are an introduction to many other variant procedures, such as monotype, rubbings, casts, block-prints.

Further themes: Rolling a Hoop; Flying a Kite; Country Dancing; My Painting and I; Sledging; Riding on a Rocking Horse; Puppet Play; At the Toyshop; Blowing Bubbles; Skipping.

SUNDAY

In the Garden Café (8-16)   A 10

> Painting in poster colours, group work. Drawing paper, pencil, box of poster colours and brush, scissors, paste or other adhesive, 4 sheets of red book-covering paper or other coloured paper.

A mural-size group-painting of a garden café necessarily consists of many smaller individual contributions. In the introductory discussion it is agreed that each child shall have a sheet of paper (about 6 inches square) on which he is to draw a party sitting at a table (round table with three chairs and three figures, left, right and centre). The proportions will be fixed by the size of the sheet: table-top halfway up the sheet, table-legs right to the bottom, figures from top to bottom. Four large sheets of book-covering paper to be joined together, two above and two below, to form an oblong used either in height or breadth, constitute the background on which the painted and cut out table groups are to be pasted. The first children to complete their table groups are given fresh sheets of paper (4 ×8 inches) on which they draw, paint and cut out small trees, to be scattered about the picture or used as a frame.

Method

The small size of the carefully measured sheet demands of each child an equally careful drawing and painting. Two figures in profile and one in full-face are to sit at the laid table. The trees are most effective if composed of simple, clearly defined

27

parts: trunks, a few clear branches with large leaves, rather than profuse foliage which would break up the unity and symmetry of the whole, even if each spray were constructed as symmetrically as the skeleton of a fish. The cutting out, the brushing of paste on the back of the paintings (to be done on sheets of newspaper) and the final pasting on to the background (press down with clean newspaper) demand equal care.

The size of the background will depend upon the number and arrangement of the individual parts. The colour red is chosen intentionally (although other colours might do), because it makes a particularly festive background for the gaily-coloured tables. The whole effect depends upon the composition. Freely rhythmic groupings can be just as attractive as strictly geometrical arrangement.

A 11 **Walk in the Woods (6-14)**

Coloured pencils, pencil or pen drawing.

The representation of the human form is one of the most important branches of art education at all ages. Fresh approaches and pretexts can always be found for this exercise, which must always be themes within a child's grasp. Children who 'can't draw people' are especially in need of new approaches to the exercise. They need above all to be encouraged to appreciate their own naive productions or at least some detail which they have mastered. Older pupils who are dissatisfied with their own work can be helped by the use of a model (a classmate) whose physical proportions they can study.

Method

The theme requires the representation of walking figures in profile. A few trees represent the wood.

We deliberately avoid painting with a brush. From the age of ten upwards, we attempt when we use exclusively linear media (pencil or pen) to develop the use of a 'pen palette'. That is to say, we examine the subjects combined in our theme to discover what different surface structures can take the place of different colours (patterns of clothing, texture of hair, bark of trees, veining of leaves). The more various the surfaces are, the more 'colourful' our picture will be, even without paint. Eventually the whole picture may be 'painted' in this way (grains of sand on the path, tufts of grass and leaves on the

28

forest floor). Even the 'flat', still sky and smooth materials can be brought to surface-life by discriminating use of dots and lines. But one can have too much of good thing. If all the surfaces speak at once, nothing will be clearly heard. Some silence is also required.

A few hints on the composition should be given: that the larger the figures, the closer they are to one another and the less empty space is left between them and the bottom of the picture, the easier it will be to unify the composition (but their feet must not reach right to the bottom but leave a certain distance in proportion to the whole). Empty spaces which remain in the picture should be filled with foreground trees. The lower the bases of these trees, the more depth will be given to the picture.

A Wedding Couple (10 upwards)   A 12

> Painting in opaque colours on a coloured ground. Drawing block, pencil, box of poster colours, brush.

There are several alternatives for this picture: the couple waving from a wedding coach or open car, entering the church in procession, surrounded by the wedding guests, or alone in a large double portrait. A good way for the teacher to find out the most promising treatment is to make a few trial sketches of various compositions himself. He will not only realise its potentialities and unforeseen pitfalls, which he might not have foreseen, but will also make sure what is realisable by his pupils and what is not. He has to keep two aims in mind: that of achieving a well unified picture and that of advancing the stage of interpretation his pupils have reached. This genuine method of art-teaching preparation will be mastered with practice.

Method

Many children will have seen a wedding couple, some will not. It is best to discuss the wedding attire and decorative detail. When the content of the picture has been decided or left optional, the children will assume that they can now start drawing as usual. This time however we must lead them to another introductory consideration, that of the colour-planning (essential only for the large double portrait).

The most important part of the bride's dress is her white veil.

It is unsatisfactory to use white paint on white paper. To use no white at all (leaving bare paper for white passages) is just as contrary to the whole idea of painting. What is to be done then? Under skilful guidance the children will find the solution for themselves: before the actual painting (better still even before drawing) they will give a medium-toned colour to the whole picture area (e.g. light blue, green, reddish-grey or greyish-orange, etc.). A medium tone is a wonderful basic harmoniser for subsequent colours as it throws up light or dark colour equally. If a large area is to be evenly covered with colour, a sufficiently large pool of opaque paint must first be prepared on the palette (lid of the paintbox). A large blob of paint is applied with a full brush along the upper edge of the slightly tilted drawing block and spread evenly downwards with frequent addition of colour. When this paint is dry the drawing can begin. In the final painting it is essential to use a rich opaque texture of paint.

Further themes: Going to Church; A Service in Church; A Car Excursion; A Picnic; An Invitation Concert; A Visit to the Zoo; Feeding the Swans; A Boat-Trip; In a Deck-chair in the Garden; At the Coffee Table.

THE WORLD OF ADOLESCENCE

A 13 **Girl at the Window (12 upwards)**

> Painting with light and shade with opaque colours. Drawing block, pencil, box of poster colours, sable brush; with a large block also bristle brush.

From 12 upwards, at latest from 14, painting in two tones (light and dark) and painting of forms in depth can be attempted. The technique is best introduced to the pupils through the demands of a particular theme; it may just as well be accepted unproblematically instead of as a difficult lesson in shaded painting. In this way the lesson may be adapted to the different needs of individual pupils. The present theme, 'Girl at the Window', is a particularly suitable one.

Method

A discussion and a direct demonstration of the action by a girl in the class recall the mental image of opening the window and

30

looking out. The back view of the figure appears dark against the bright background of the world outside and is at the same time edged with light which laps gently round it, so that the deepest shadow remains only at the centre of the head, neck and back. The parts of the wall surrounding the window also lie in shade and so are in strong contrast to the highest light of the window opening. We aim then at a dark-framed picture at the centre of which a dark figure stands against a light ground, its form modelled by the light.

The picture is best painted on a large block with the large figure in the foreground, head, hair, clothes in simple outline. During the drawing, we lay particular stress upon a good, simple rendering of the hands which are apt to be drawn too small; they must not be hidden but must rest on the frame of the open window. Each painter may draw the view from his own house or one from imagination. In order to advance towards painting in the round, we start by concentrating on a simple and easily comprehensible detail, such as the girl's hair. Our aim is to make the transition from dark to light, from inwards outwards in imperceptible gradations, so that no blotches, lines of drying or sudden changes in the shades of colour are allowed to occur. It is an exercise in manual dexterity, in brushcraft and in the use of the palette. The white is worked in with gentle, spreading or dotting brushstrokes (possibly with a bristle brush, almost 'dry' painting). Not until this first detail is successfully completed should anything else be undertaken. To achieve a really strong contrast between the inner and outer parts of the picture, all the colours may, if necessary, be mixed with either white or black.

Sitting in the Park (15 upwards) A 14

> Lino cut (see *150 Techniques in Art,* p. 57). Piece of lino, cutting tool, rubber roller, pane of glass, printing colour, absorbent paper for printing, old newspaper.

By a theme of the world of adolescence I mean one which allows a young boy or girl to give artistic expression to particular aspects of his or her own experience. One may give indirect stimulus to such self-expression through the formula 'Two People' (with titles such as: Sitting in the Park, Conversation, Two's Company, A Walk in the Woods, etc.). Such a general formula allows a definite personal choice not only of content but also of technique and composition.

Method

The representation of the human form is no problem to older pupils if human subjects have already been approached in numerous different ways throughout the earlier years. This is not always the case however. Since the artistic value of a work does not depend upon the stage of the artist's development and valid work can be done at every stage, it follows that the un-practised draughtsman must simply begin honestly, bravely and in earnest at whatever stage he has actually reached. In other words, he must freely accept the naivety and crudeness of his own unstudied work and must not at first make demands upon himself which he cannot fulfil. The frank resolve to do this is not an easy one for an adolescent, and only the teacher's real faith in the value of all honest self-expression can inspire him to make it.

The design for our lino cut (made on a separate piece of paper) demands of the pupil nothing more or less than a com-pletely honest drawing (Plate 3a). A drawing is honest if every line makes a factual statement and never pretends. Inevitable defects in the drawing (e.g. confused scratches for drapery, ingenious scrawls for foliage, surface structures or hatching, ill-observed anatomical detail) can easily be replaced by simpler lines based on definite observation, to the great enhancement of the whole picture. A design thus strictly simplified is always suitable for cutting on to the lino. If, when the single line has been cut, a black-on-white print is required, the simplest method is to cut away everything except the figures or objects in the picture with a U-shaped gouge.

A 15 **Couples Dancing (13 upwards)**

> Painting with a limited range of colours. Drawing block, pencil, box of poster colours with tube of white and sable brush.

Adolescent children need not only particular themes of art, beyond those which they share with all age-groups, but also different modes of expression. The child's naive delight in bright colours gradually gives place to a feeling for subtleties of colour. Painting with a restricted palette is an essential method of encouraging colour sensitivity at this stage. Often,

32

the fewer the colours chosen for a painting, the more impressive the final result. A picture in one colour is possible only if it is used not only pure (without any admixture) but with contrast from high-lights to deepest shadows, that is to say, lightened with white and darkened with black ('simple' light and shade painting). A further possibility, mixing with white and black simultaneously, producing the various shades of grey from white to black, enriches the restricted palette considerably. The discovery of the full scale of possibilities of a single colour can be made only through the use of a restricted palette.

Method

Our theme is 'Dancing Lesson' or 'Couples Dancing', and we are to concentrate on a few couples for our painting in which they will be large foreground figures. If we decide to use the length of our paper vertically, the figures will be brought close together to form a closely knit composition. A certain depth is given by smaller background figures and some overlapping of the foreground couples. This is a stepping stone towards an interest in spatial representation.

The use of the colour here is very important. Any arbitrary changes from light to dark must be warned against and a carefully planned use of contrast demanded. The simplest way is to give each figure, or better still, each couple, a definite tone-value so that they stand out in spatial relation to other couples with a different tone-value (the foreground couples relatively dark, the furthest couples lightest). The parts of the picture left free, the background and floor of the room, are best painted in a uniform tone against which the other colours stand out either dark or light.

Further themes: My Friend and I; A Duet; Outside the Shop-Window; At the Theatre; Lost in the Forest; Round the Camp-Fire; Self-portrait Reading; Sunbathing; Camping; Dreaming in the Moonlight.

B THE SOCIAL ENVIRONMENT

PUBLIC HOLIDAY

B1 **Roundabout with Horses (all ages)**

> Painting with poster colours. Drawing block, pencil, box of poster colours, brush.

Fairs are a delight to children and a feast to the eye. Round-abouts, swing-boats, big wheels, what a wealth of pictures! The Roundabout is one of the chief attractions of the fair-ground. Great painters have found delight in it. From schoolchildren of all ages the theme calls forth a sumptuous array of paintings (Plate 3b).

Method

Rightly to introduce a new task is to prepare a new experience for the pupil. This is the test of the teacher's ability to awaken and foster first enthusiasm and clear understanding.

There are three chief methods of introduction, depending on the subject chosen. One may appeal to the free imagination of the class by a discussion of the forms and enactment of the gestures (e.g. with the subjects: The Enchanted Castle, A Mermaid, Fantastic Ships); or one may clarify an already exist-ing visual image (e.g. The Fair, Our Postman, A Cockfight) by analytical discussion; or one can create new visual images by looking at and discussing the pictorial possibilities of man-made or natural objects to be portrayed (Geranium, Canterbury Cathedral, Mrs Smith's Cat).

According to the artistic and technical demands of the task, a further practical introduction is needed. It should consist of clear pointers as to the 'how', in the physical and manual sense. A successful and educational piece of work is impossible with-out such pointers; perplexity, boredom, mechanicalness and every form of laziness will supervene if they are not given. The pupil must have a clear and stimulating experience not only of a planned way of working but also of the concentration and pleasures in the work which are essential for its success. The teacher must also inculcate in his pupils the careful consider-

34

Plate 3

a   Sitting in the Park (A14), lino cut, by a 16-year-old girl. Width 20 inches

b   Roundabout with Horses (B1), in poster colours, by an 11-year-old boy.
Width 24 inches

Plate 4

*a   Switchback (B2), plaster relief, by a student teacher.
Width 34 inches*

*b   Putting the Shot (B5), foil painting,
by a 13-year-old boy. Height 88 inches*

c   Ski Expedition (B6), lino cut, by a 13-year-old girl. Width 18 inches

Plate I

Self-portrait (A1), in poster-colours, by a 10-year-old girl. Height 20 inches

ation necessary to the construction of the picture, for instance, as to the size of the objects, the division of the picture area and balance of the colour. For this explanatory drawings on the blackboard by the teacher are only occasionally necessary: they should simply be rough indications and should be rubbed out again immediately.

Switchback (all ages) B 2

A plaster picture (see *150 Technique in Art,* p. 38). Four boards for an improvised frame, 16×20 inches base, hammer, 4 nails, newspaper, plaster of Paris, 2 large bowls, penknife, pencil, box of poster colours, brush, small bottle of oil-varnish.

It is possible to draw and paint just as well on a surface of plaster poured into a temporary wooden frame as on paper. The actual experience however is quite different and the final effect is similar to that of a painting on stone. A preliminary sketch with pencil and paper is afterwards scratched with a penknife or nail on the plaster. Two coats of varnish, applied after painting, give a splendid glaze to the colours. The first coat closes the surface and must dry completely before the second is applied.

Method

The complex structure of a switchback with its many intersections and perspective foreshortenings may appear to be too difficult a subject for schoolchildren to draw. The experienced teacher knows that these difficulties do not daunt a young child, who represents objects symbolically and draws without regard to technical or perspective problems. Older pupils will be helped by the reminder that in art a different kind of rightness is required than in nature drawing. A switchback which, as it is depicted, could never really work but which decorates the surface with beautiful curves and provides a feast for the eye is 'right' (Plate 4a). Its function is not technical but pictorial. Children who are a little inhibited need only some help with the analysis of the complex subject; this is nearly always true in such cases. The teacher should concentrate their attention exclusively on the sweeping curves of the picture. Next the curves must be widened into tracks and supplied with safety rails. Not until then are the supporting girders to be added. Last of all come the passengers hurrying to the paybox, getting into the carriages, coasting up and down the steep inclines. Flags and pennants, garlands and attractive signboards add to the gaiety of the picture.

B 3 The Little Orchestra (all ages)

> Painting in poster colours or lino-cut (as B1 or A9); also lino rubbing or plaster cast from the lino-cut (see *150 Techniques in Art*, pp. 58 and 70).

If a relief block (lino or wood) has large, simple figures which either stand out as a so-called black-on-white cut or are cut away to produce a white-on-black cut, a rubbed print, as well as the normal lino print, can be taken from it. Just as children make rubbings of coins by covering them with paper and rubbing a pencil across the raised design, they can make graphite or wax crayon rubbings of these simple lino cuts. White-line and white-on-black lino cuts are also suitable for making plaster casts. Plaster is poured into an improvised wooden frame fitted round the edges of the lino plate. No preparation of the lino is necessary as the smooth plaster comes away easily. The cast will have either raised lines or planes. If the plate was previously painted with a dark colour (with ink, poster or powder colour) the stain can easily be rubbed off the plaster with glass-paper. The result is an effective relief picture.

Method

The conductor in front of his orchestra of string and wind instrumentalists is an impressive figure. Since the orchestra need not be large, the subject is a good exercise in composition. The bows of the violins in a well rehearsed orchestra move as one. This we will show in our picture. The rhythmic repetition of gestures in a picture delights the eye, whereas a multiplicity of disconnected movements merely bewilder it. There must be no 'gaps' in the picture to left or right of the conductor, so we will decide to place the musicians as near as possible to the lower edges of the picture, to the conductor and to one another. Figure compositions of this kind are just as suitable themes for painting on paper as for wood or lino cuts.

Further themes: Swing-boats; The Big Wheel; The Balloon-Seller; Torchlight Procession; Puppet Theatre; A Circus Act; Juggler with Balls.

40

SPORT

A Race (all ages)

> Painting in poster colours. Drawing block, pencil, box of poster colours, brush.

The theme chosen is deliberately not confined to one particular kind of race, but is intended as a comprehensive title. The pupils are offered a wide choice, from the 100 yards to a horse race, dog race, car race, yacht race, or even an air race. The purpose of this freedom is that from ten upwards pupils should learn to dispose of the picture area and compose their picture with particular regard to the content chosen. Since each individual choice of subject cannot be discussed beforehand with the whole class, we must stress that each pupil is to compose his own picture and to give great attention to the task.

Method

Since watching a race and even taking part in it is an intensely dramatic experience which every child has had, the class will start with a lively exchange of impressions. Even the enumeration of all the possible kinds of race arouses excitement. Someone asks whether a climbing race can be counted, or even a beetle race. Then comes the difficult moment of choosing from such a wealth of possibilities. At length the transference of ideas to paper begins. Some children come to a quick decision, others still hesitate. The next stage is reached when everyone, concentrating on his own idea, has shown by his pencil drawing how far he can succeed in transforming what he remembers or imagines into a good picture. Boldly imaginative pictures may succeed just as well as those based on familiar scenes. Each child inevitably reveals his own nature in his drawing.

If, in the course of the work, the class has a look at the promising starts already made, ambition is spurred on. It is also a help if the teacher makes a regular round of the class to get some out of unnecessary difficulties and to stop others wasting time on insincere scribbles. The final appreciation of all the pictures by the class and the teacher is indispensable. The anticipation of this audience is a stimulus, though usually an unconscious one, throughout the task.

Giant Figure: Putting the Shot (12 upwards)

Gold and Silver Leaf painting, group work (see *150 Techniques in Art*, p. 82). Packing paper, charcoal, powder colours, foil, oil-varnish, bristle brush.

Our classroom, the school hall or the gymnasium needs large mural decorations. We are going to emulate Myron, creator of the celebrated 'Discus Thrower', by creating a figure putting the shot. We begin with a competition for the best design in which everyone takes part. We are our own jury. Each design is pinned to the board and its particular qualities considered. Finally everyone votes for his favourite design. The one with the most votes is the winner. Now comes the test as to whether this design or another is best suited for translation into a foil painting. As the class does not yet know the technique, the teacher has the casting vote. The most suitable design is the one which most clearly represents the action of putting the shot in large, simple and unforeshortened forms (Plate 4b).

Method

We pin a sheet of packing paper of the required size to the wall so that it reaches the floor. The enlargement of the design is drawn freehand without any mechanical aids in charcoal. When this drawing is satisfactorily completed, it is gone over with a brush drawing in ink or powder colour. Next each separate area of the figure is marked with pencil to indicate its intended colour. (Figure—gold and silver; background—a plain coat of powder paint of a suitable colour.)

Since the whole class is to take part in the ensuing stages of the work, we divide the picture up like a chessboard into as many numbered areas as there are pupils. Each pupil begins by brushing varnish (with a bristle brush) over the parts of his sector which are to be covered with foil, without covering the lines of the figure which are to be visible in the final picture. The thin sheets of foil are next applied and the background afterwards painted over with powder colour. The main work of making this large cartoon is finished in a comparatively short time. When it is dry (within 24 hours) any untidy edges of foil are trimmed off and the separate sectors reassembled. The simplest way is to paste them all on to a second sheet of packing paper. The finished picture, its edges bound and strengthened with strips of gummed paper, can be fixed to the wall by a few pins.

Ski Expedition (10 upwards)

> Large lino cut (see *150 Techniques in Art*, p. 57). Piece of lino, cutting tool, pane of glass, rubber roller, printing colour, absorbent paper, newspaper.

The theme 'sport', like all generalised themes, is also a comprehensive theme like 'A Race' and can be used in the same way (see B4), subdivided into field sports, winter sports, indoor sports, etc. The theme for our lino cut can be given in the narrow sense as 'A Ski Expedition' (Plate 4c) or in a general sense as 'Skiing' and it would be possible to leave each pupil to choose and develop his own subordinate theme independently.

Method

We start by sketching our ideas on paper. The pupil will not design as for a lino cut without some prompting from the teacher. Only experienced designers are able to feel their subject at this stage in relation to the intended medium, to adapt it to the texture of the medium and to the area at their disposal. The method of 'framing' helps to overcome this problem. Certain successful parts of one or more designs can be isolated or combined; they can either be 'framed' alone or together into a new composition which is designed to 'close' a rectangle of the dimensions of the lino plate, that is, to leave no meaningless, empty space within it. Its transference (in pencil) to the lino strips down the design into as clear and terse a statement as possible; the rhythmic repetition of significant lines is a good means of achieving clarity. Large lino plates allow the use of two or more colours for the print.

Further themes: Wrestlers; Boys or Girls Playing Leap-Frog; Knee-hanging from the Horizontal Bar; Rope-Climbing; A Horse Race; Pyramid of Acrobats; On the High-Diving Board; Ice-skating; The Trick-Cyclist; Football Goal.

OCCUPATION

The Vinegrower (10 upwards)

> Painting in poster colours. Drawing block, pencil, box of poster colours, brush.

Before he can assume that the average pupil will carry out this task successfully, the teacher must ask himself three questions:

1. Does this theme interest the pupils as a picture?
2. Have they a vivid visual image of it?
3. Is the task completely within the pupil's capacity?

We must not omit one further condition of success, which is a fundamental requirement of every theme of art and the most difficult to check, at least for the inexperienced teacher; this requirement is that the theme should be capable of pictorial interpretation. A theme is not pictorial unless its essential components can form a compositional unity within a given picture area (e.g. Laocoon, Girl at the Window, Basket of Fruit, and all themes given here). Subjects which are based exclusively on non-pictorial ideas (literary or scientific) often do not satisfy this requirement (e.g. Sportsman Shooting a Fieldfare at 300 yards; The Remains of the Roman Wall . . . .; Voyage from Gibraltar to India).

Method

First Step: To produce a vivid mental image of the subject, tell the fairy tale of the poor vinegrower who possessed only two vines and harvested a bunch of golden grapes.

Second Step: Study the characteristics of a vine-leaf, count and name its parts, the veining, the curves and indentations of its outline.

Third Step: Narrow the subject down from the grape-harvest to the vinegrower with two vines. Concentration can be further increased if necessary by division of the task into successive stages. When the drawing is finished, the first task might be to paint only one of the carefully drawn leaves in its autumn colours, as delicately as possible, before starting on the second leaf. Such disciplines introduced by the teacher lead to self-discipline. The complex shapes of the objects in the picture will make it difficult to paint the background of sky afterwards, so we either paint the whole background before drawing or leave the paper as background.

B 8 Saxophonists (10 upwards)

> Wire picture (see *150 Techniques in Art*, p. 88). Wooden boards, nails, all kinds of wire, hammer, pliers.

There are various methods of making a wire picture. We choose a flat montage of wire lines (based on a drawing the same size as our picture) upon the background of a wide-meshed piece of wire netting in a wooden frame. Only a small group of children can work at the same time on this kind of picture. The rest of the class may either do some other work or be divided into similar groups each with its own wire picture frame.

Method

To obtain a suitable design, we have a competition for the best drawing of 'Saxophonists'. The best pictures are then redrawn to the required scale in charcoal and laid under the framed wire netting. The montage is begun by bending and flattening out the coarser wire to correspond with the outlines of the figures in the charcoal design (Plate 5 a). With the fine wire we fix down these outlines at intervals on to the netting. When all the lines of the design have been repeated in wire, the figures can be 'dressed' or 'painted', if we like. This is done by 'weaving' across and across the figures with wire, making them stand out better from the background, and giving 'colour' to our picture.

The Pastry Cook's Shop (all ages, esp. 10-13) B 9

Painting in poster colours. Drawing block, pencil, box of poster paints, brush.

The problem of choosing a theme is an ever-present one. It is not even enough if a subject satisfies the two essential conditions that it should be suitable for the pupils and promise them success, that is, that it should be both valid for a child and valid pictorially (see A 3). A theme should also be the right link between the previous task and the one which is to follow, a transition and a development. No fixed rules can be laid down for achieving this sequence, yet any arbitrary choice of a task without regard to sequence must be unconstructive. In reality the right choice is the outcome of a teacher's sympathetic feeling for the class's direction of development and is thus dictated by the pulse of the class itself.

Any small boy or girl is excited at the prospect of a feast of cakes and pastries. How wonderful it must be to be a master baker and to spend one's whole life among biscuits, doughnuts and meringues. Wearing his tall white hat, a white apron and a beaming smile, he stands behind his counter surrounded by his precious wares. What a gay and inviting image!

45

Method

Our task is to turn this image into a picture. The master baker will be a half-length figure, as large as possible (the paper to be used in height); his hands rest on the counter where just enough space is left between the pastries. The splendid array which surrounds him fills the rest of the picture. It may be drawn first with brush or pencil and afterwards painted in poster colours. Alternatively the colour masses may be painted in first and a dark brush-line drawing superimposed to reveal the detail. Brush drawing in light colours (either mixed with white or pure white for the cream) can also be added subsequently to reveal the structure and decorative detail. A rich, gay picture will result.

The pork butcher wielding his chopper, surrounded by rows of hams and festoons of sausages, could be the central figure of another mouth-watering picture.

Further themes: Flowerseller; Chimney-Sweep; Our Postman; A Builder; Mending Fishing Nets; Train Conductor; Painter in his Studio; Chemist in his Laboratory; Gardner in his Greenhouse; The First Chorister.

TECHNICAL ENVIRONMENT

B 10 **The Concrete Mixer (all ages)**

> Coloured pencil or pen drawing. Oil or wax crayons, coloured pencil or ball-point pen, fountain pen or drawing pen and ink, possibly felt pen or any graphic medium.

Wherever new building is in progress, a concrete-mixer adds to the din. A giant shovel scoops up sand and gravel, is raised high into the air by a mysterious mechanism, tips its whole load down the gullet of the monster, whose revolving maw digests everything. Look, a jet of water to slake its thirst! Suddenly rods and levers begin to move and the great belly throws itself forward and disgorges its meal into the waiting conveyor. The question for the artist is: can this scene, watched by a child, be transformed into a picture which is both childlike and artistically valid in itself? Is not some specialised knowledge of the mechanism essential to its portrayal, or is it something quite different that justifies a picture? The answer is not to be found by intellectual speculation, or even through intuitive sympathy with the mind of a child. The answer is given by experience, by the power of the child's own activity to persuade us. His carefree treatment of the subject decides us. The simple clarity of his picture answers the questions without ambiguity. What really matters is something quite other than technical understanding. It is intuitive transformation of visual experience into a picture. That is what makes a picture so 'right' that it cannot have 'mistakes' in it. All the experience symbolised in the picture was right because it was physiognomic, whole and complete.

Method

Hence there is a very good preparation for the drawing of technical equipment. When they have seen the external appearance and movement of a machine, children know it as a rhythmic motif, as a thing that moves. If only we will provide impressions of things in motion, children are capable of representing them pictorially. Older pupils can approach such subjects with technical interest as well. As this new kind of interest is genuine and natural to their age, it is right to discuss such subjects from a technical point of view with boys of 12 upwards. They will attempt to do justice to their logical and technical grasp of the subject in their drawings, and we shall find that this approach also allows of artistic expression and does not diminish the artistic value of the results. They will not be any better or worse than the naive earlier versions, merely different. The danger of getting bogged down in a sterile rationalistic and scientific constructivism does not normally exist for the young.

The Fire Brigade (all ages)   B 11

> Painting in poster colour or gouache on dark paper. Drawing block, or dark paper, or black or dark cardboard, pencil, box of poster colours with tube of white, sable brush.

Certain themes suggest themselves for painting in opaque colour on a coloured ground. The subject, 'The Fire Brigade Fighting a Fire at Night', is filled with dramatic and pictorial interest. From the teacher's point of view, it is an opportunity to use opaque paint in brilliant colours (flames, jets of water) against a dark ground (night) which the pupils can appreciate

(Plate 5 b). This presupposes the use of thick paint, which with older pupils can lead to a new technique, gouache-painting, in which all the colours are rendered luminous by the admixture of white.

Method

If no dark paper (poster board, cardboard, etc.) is available, we must prepare on our palettes (lid of the paintbox) a sufficient quantity of strong dark colour to cover the whole background of our drawing block. When this coat is dry, a pencil drawing may be used to compose the picture: rows of houses, flames bursting from their roofs and windows, people crowding up and, above all, the red fire-engine, its ladders extended, hoses spouting. This varied and animated scene can be tackled in a variety of ways. The youngest pupils will be illustrating a story and even older groups may be left free to follow their enthusiasm for the exciting subject and the new technique. At the same time, more advanced pupils might plan and compose a more exacting picture, such as a concentration of the fire theme upon a figure jumping into a life-saving sheet.

B 12 Industrial Picture (8 upwards)

Wax engraving (see *150 Techniques in Art*, p. 37). Drawing block, wax crayons, drawing ink, penknife. (Also other techniques.)

Technical 'landscapes' composed of blast-furnaces, pylons, cranes and excavators possess the charm of the bizarre. The theme 'industry' covers a wide field, from a harmless, almost romantic brickyard to the dreamlike surrealistic spectral impression of a nuclear power station (Colour Plate II). There is a genealogy of interest in these things which starts early when children watch excitedly while an excavator churns up the ground. Later they gaze spellbound by the idea of the inner laws which govern the technological world.

This store of visual images, which belongs to every child, can be brought to life by a few stimulating words from the teacher and by the interest of a suitable technique, and turned into pictures which satisfy the child's desire to express his own experience in tangible forms.

Method

The technique of wax engraving consists of the following processes: first, we cover the paper with a thick layer of wax

48

colour (white, yellow, red, blue, green), so that neither the paper nor any separate line of wax is visible. A second dark layer of wax (brown or black) is applied over this and is the layer to be engraved. It can, if necessary, be replaced by a coat of drawing ink (or poster paint). As the first layer of wax is fast to the paper, it will be left visible if the top layer is scratched away with a suitable tool (penknife, nail-file, etc.). The engraving can be in the form of lines or areas. For this particular subject we can vary the colour of the basic layer at random, unless we prefer to use a single colour. Other themes demand foresight as to the intended colour and placing of the various objects in the engraving. However one should not be too precise or over-anxious about this, since the effect of some accidental colour changes can often be very attractive.

Further themes: Aerials and Radar-Station; Forest of Pylons; Shipping with Cranes; Signal-Box and Signals; Engine-Room; Conveyor Belts; Landscape with Gasometers; Winding Towers; A Rocket Station.

TRAFFIC

The Bus Stop (all ages)   B 13

> Painting in poster colour. Drawing block, pencil, box of poster colours, brush.

The larger the drawing block used (ideal size 22 ×18 inches), the earlier a direct, unalterable brush line can be usefully introduced as the basis of the picture. The fact that lines cannot be corrected has a wonderfully liberating effect upon artistically inhibited children (and adults). If the initial fear of this new medium is once got over by a single bold decision to accept it, its loosening effect is felt at once. The need to amend simply disappears. Moreover a large scale of drawing has the obvious virtue of offering wider scope to the pupil's capacities. This greater breadth of drawing appeals to and satisfies the child's motor instincts. Single-figure subjects give full opportunity to use the scope afforded by a large sheet, while multi-figure subjects absolutely demand it.

Method

Several people are standing at the bus stop and crowding into

49

the bus, which is almost full. This is the scene we are to represent. It suggests horizontal use of the picture space. On the left is the open door of the bus. Along the upper edge of the picture, like little, separately framed pictures, are the figures of the passengers seen through the windows. In proportion to their size, the size of the large foreground figures will be fixed. Of course some children will want to draw the whole bus instead of only a section of it, and, the younger they are, the more natural is this desire. Young children cannot yet understand the idea of limitation of the subject.

When the drawing is completed, painting can be started. At this juncture, a check should be made as to whether everyone has used his imagination to the full. What a detailed story can be told of all that is going on, about those who are waiting to get on the bus, those who have managed to board it, and those who are still at the end of the line. This narrative aspect of the theme should be fully exploited.

B 14 **A Bicycling Accident (10 upwards)**

> Mural-size painting in powder colours, group work, on packing paper. Roll of packing paper, charcoal, powder colours, bristle brush. (Also as an individual work on a smaller scale. Drawing block, box of poster colours, brush.)

It is only a fall from the bike and a few bruises; nothing serious. All the more exciting is the tumbling confusion of cycles and riders. If a large enough roll of paper is provided, the colliding and tumbling bicycles and the boys and girls riding them can be almost life-size.

Method

Two or three draughtsmen at a time come to the wall to which the cartoon is pinned. (The rest of the class does some other work.) They each make a large charcoal sketch of a rider and his bicycle. Then a fresh team take their places and add more cyclists in suitable spaces in the picture. When the picture needs no further addition, the painting can be started. As the theme of bicycles is an occasion rather for drawing than for painting, a brush drawing can dominate the picture, wherever it can be used to clarify the forms.

Direct painting in poster colours. Drawing block, box of poster colours, brush.

Written accounts of class excursions are frequently demanded by the English teacher. If the school has an excursion album, there is never any lack of illustration for it. We discover from the visitors' books of Youth Hostels the existence of a special effusive style of art, which here celebrates its orgies of insipidity. The teacher must make the distinction quite clear between what is being done in class and such caricatures of art and sentimental rubbish. The younger children express their experience spontaneously and are therefore immune from such dangerous influences. It is the classes of the middle and upper school whose attempts at illustrative work easily deteriorate into a mass-produced pseudo-picture of the world, succumbing to spiritless commercialism or the latest derivative mode. Themes taken from experience therefore demand particular vigilance on the part of the teacher.

First the choice of the exact subject requires care. Illustrative demands must never be so exacting as to stifle the creative urge. In other words, the theme must be simple and at the same time promising for a picture.

Method

'Our Steamboat Carries Us up the Rhine' is the full title of the picture. It is formulated so as to give definite bounds to the pictorial idea, concentrating it on a single viewpoint. This viewpoint has its own horizon and so prevents the composition becoming diffuse. Moreover the actual centre of the experience, the group of children contained within the boat, being the very core of the subject, dictates its own limits, its own 'frame'. The surrounding landscape (the flowing river, even the craggy shoreline) cannot endanger the concentration of the picture.

We can therefore paint directly, since all is clear and within our range of vision, definitely limited, and, in this broad medium (brush instead of pencil), can readily be reduced to greater simplicity as work goes on, without spoiling the effect.

Further themes: The Traffic Warden; In the Station Hall; An Airport; A Balloon Ascent; In the Forest of Traffic Lights; The Dump for Old Cars; Caterpillar Tractors; A Traffic Roundabout in the Rush-Hour; Ships Entering and Leaving a Port; At the Filling Station.

C THE NATURAL AND ARCHITECTURAL ENVIRONMENT

STILL LIFE

C 1   Cakes and Pastries (10 upwards)

> Painting in poster colours. Drawing block, pencil, box of poster colours, brush.

In art teaching there are so-called 'trump' subjects that always yield good results. The professional art-teacher knows all about these somewhat overworked themes and is not particularly addicted to them if he is a vital teacher. 'Cocks' and 'Fish' belong to this category as do 'Pastries' and 'Basket of Fruit'. It is important to realise that children approach them quite differently. The teacher's dislike of repetition or imitation of others must not deprive his pupils of a worthwhile experience of artistic achievement. The teacher's task is to approach the theme with such freshness and immediacy that not only his pupils but he himself sees it as if for the first time.

Method

Are not birthday tea-tables and sweetshop counters initially a feast for the eye? Why not feast our eyes on painted pastries if we need an alluring subject for the art class? Would it not be a worthwhile achievement to paint a strawberry tart that really made our mouths water, a cream cake at the sight of which we actually tasted the cream or hazelnut meringues that made us long to bite off a crunchy mouthful? Such is the delightful ambition that spurs the class at the outset.

Our poster paints can be used to decorate the pastries in a realistic manner. A cherry tart, for instance, can be decorated with a circle of white cream straight from the paintbox, and the pink, yellow and white layers of cream in certain elaborate pieces of confectionery can be given a realistic rich, creamy texture with poster paint. How highly we value the mere sight of such delicacies is revealed in the final piping with the icing syringe. We will not forget this last essential artistic touch.

Drinking Goblets (15 upwards) C 2

Paper mosaic in black, white and grey. Drawing block, box of poster colours, brush, scissors, paste or other adhesive, newspaper, pencil.

A good shop window decorator achieves his effect not by heaping together a collection of heterogeneous objects, but by using one and the same object ten or even 30 times and cleverly composing it into a rhythmic pattern pleasing to the eye. In the same way the senior classes can practise composing still-life pictures in which individually descriptive detail is sacrificed in favour of a deliberately planned arrangement of the basic forms of the subject (Colour Plate IV). Many household and natural objects lend themselves to this treatment by the characteristic simplicity of their forms—vases, drinking glasses, bottles, shells, bulbs (see J 10-12).

Method

The true starting point of our creative work should be direct experience of the particular beauty of line of a goblet. Thence the wish should arise to commemorate the experience by translating its beauty into a picture. We may start with a large simple pencil drawing in which the lines of the goblet are rhythmically repeated. We may then translate it into a paper mosaic, restricting our palette to a colour-scale of greys (Plate 6 a). We produce our own paper 'tiles', painting them and cutting them out. The application of the tiles is the second important creative process. The choice of colour-gradations and contrasts, the precision of the symmetrical fugal treatment, the cutting of the tiles ($2\frac{1}{2}$ square inches) to conform exactly with the outlines of the goblets all demand absolute concentration.

Large Basket of Fruit (8 upwards) C 3

Painting in coloured black-board chalks on a large sheet of packing paper, or on 'kitchen' paper, sugar paper, shelf paper, etc.; group work.

This kind of group work by a whole class presupposes that the majority of the class is occupied meanwhile with some other task. Only two or three children at a time come up to the large sheet of paper pinned to the wall or board to begin or continue the group-work. The pupils may change places either at will or at prearranged intervals (of about 5 minutes). In this way all the members of the class contribute, in turn or in their own order, to the communal picture which is gradually filled up and completed.

Method

When we look at the finished production, it is scarcely possible to detect how or where the work was begun. The uninitiated often do not even guess that so many different people have combined to produce it. Actually Frank drew the first line when he sketched in the outline of the great bowl of the basket, and his sister put in the first pear. Hannah started the basket-work by painting the perpendicular lines all round it, through which Cilla and Anita painted the intertwining horizontal lines. Meanwhile other children had drawn in apples, grapes and cherries and coloured them carefully. It was Charlotte who finally discovered the possibility of colouring the bowl of the basket as well. When it seemed to be almost finished, Anne had the good idea of putting a frame round the whole picture, and Edith added the last strokes.

Further themes: A Net Shopping Bag; Toys; Coffee- or Tea-Things; The Open Jewel Box; A Mountain of Boxes and Trunks; Onions and Pumpkins; Electric Light Bulbs; An Open Wardrobe; A Full Fishing Net; A Package of Books.

PLANTS

C 4   **Vase of Flowers (all ages)**

> Painting in poster colours. Drawing block, box of poster colours, brush.

Splendid pictures are inspired by splendid subjects. That the beauty of flowers has always captivated the painter's eye, is testified by beautiful flower paintings of many periods in the history of art. It has been left to this century to add to all this praise the eternally fresh vision of children.

Method

We decide that our picture is to be of a vase with a large bouquet of flowers, but that we are going to be more concerned with evoking the splendour of the colour than with representing the individual plants exactly. We are to paint the flowers as a

54

Plate II

Industrial Picture (B 12), wax engraving, by a 17-year-old girl. Width 22 inches

Plate 5

b The Fire Brigade (B11), in poster colours, by a student
teacher. Height 24 inches

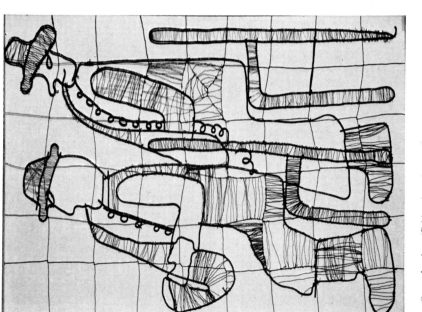

a Saxophonists (B8), wire picture, by a 15-year-old boy.
Height 38 inches

Plate 6

a   Drinking Goblets (C2), paper mosaic, by a student teacher. Width 24 inches

b   Patch of Field Grass (C5), silhouette, by a student teacher. Width 22 inches

bouquet, not as a selection of different kinds of flowers. It can therefore flow quite freely from our general conception of flowers. Our painting technique follows from this aim: we shall apply large 'splashed' areas of colour directly on to our paper (used vertically), wherever we want them, without any preliminary drawing. We shall paint brilliant flowers surrounded by the light or dark green of the leaves, and the vase itself as a larger mass of colour until the whole picture space is completely covered with paint (Plate 7a). It is quite likely that adjacent colours will run into each other if they are still wet; the surplus colour must be mopped up sufficiently to prevent a muddy effect. When the paint has dried, the second stage of the picture begins: the whole bouquet of flowers is brush-drawn with strong opaque colour. The light and dark lines of the drawing are to divide and give distinct form to what was hitherto a crude and comparatively vague riot of colour, to give definite outline to flowers and to leaves their rounded or serrated edges. This drawing should not follow slavishly the fortuitous outlines of the splashes of colour, but contribute a new life of its own. (Younger children invent their own way of painting. From about 10 years of age they can be introduced to this technique of splashed colour followed by brush drawing.)

Patch of Field Grass (10 upwards) C 5

> Large silhouette. Drawing block, pencil, scissors, box of poster colours, brush, adhesive paste or gum.

There are various ways of producing a silhouette. Direct cutting is the initial and also the final step in the series of procedures. Nevertheless there exist remarkable examples by peasant artists and also by well-known artists which were first outlined in pencil. It remains true to say that anyone who does not also cut out while drawing produces at best a cut-out drawing, not a true silhouette. The essential features of a genuine silhouette are: a perfectly clear outline (i.e. silhouette, since there is no question of inner drawing, at any rate not at first) and sharp, pointed outlines in cut-out style (not a naturalistic imitation of apparent outlines or of anatomy, nor of perspective and depth). Since the drawings of young children have the simplicity of parables and are unconcerned with naturalism, they lend themselves directly to transformation into silhouettes by simple cutting out. Later this simplicity has to some extent to be relearnt by many pupils.

Method

Before starting an exercise it is essential to envisage both the result aimed at and the whole process by which it is to be achieved. In this case we may either cut out the field grasses and plants separately and combine them later to form a patch of grass, or cut out a patch of turf with which they form one whole. In either case we must avoid all intersection or over-lapping and give the plants a symbolic, generalised form rather than a realistic, accidental one (Plate 6b); in other words, we must work from a visual image or even from free imagination.

For the cutting we do not need any special silhouette paper; a sheet from the drawing block will do. When it is finished we paste it with a few dabs of paste to a background sheet which we have coloured ourselves. In the case of delicate complex silhouettes, it is best to paste down the central parts first and to hold up the 'excrescent' parts and paste each one down separately with light dabs of paste.

C 6 **Cacti (10 upwards)**

> Painting in poster colours. Drawing block, pencil, box of poster colours, brush.

The Socratic method of teaching, called 'the art of midwifery' which was handed on by Plato and extolled especially in his *Meno*, was based on the conviction that we can learn nothing that we have not always known and that learning is simply remembering.

A true teacher of art is always practising midwifery in this sense. His midwifery consists of inducing his pupils to give birth to all the stored treasure of their visual experience and in drawing from them a delightful picture on his chosen theme, by piecing together, like mosaic tiles, the many tiny fragments of the knowledge that each individual already possesses, in order to create the richly coloured whole. So it is with our picture of eacti.

When at last all these characters, the smooth shiny ones, the short bristly fellows, the pleated, the scaly, the prickly and the hairy stand before the mind's eye and stretch forth the flames of their spearlike blossoms and unfold the delicate glory

60

of their silken heads, the class will, under the teacher's guidance and yet individually and actively, have experienced what 'movement' in the plant world means, will have paid homage to it and grasped what this theme demands of them.

Method

A piece of creative work prepared in this way is sufficiently based on artistic perception from within. The pictures produced will be symbols of Nature working from within, and do not need the orientation of a particular external subject. They are at the same time symbols of the individual's self-expression, standing for the soul of the painter conceiving and bringing forth pictures. This guidance is indeed no more than a leading back into remembered experience. The treasure lies there waiting to be uncovered. Our task is to give our minds to it and to make use of it.

Further themes: Apple-tree in Blossom; The Hot-House; Corner of the Garden; A Flowerbed in Spring; Potted Plants on a Windowsill; Garland of Flowers; Fruit-Trees against a Wall; Palms in a Conservatory; A Flowering Branch; A Basket of Flowers.

ANIMALS

Cockfight (all ages)   C 7

> Painting in poster colours. Drawing block, pencil, box of poster colours, brush.

This is a particularly promising subject for children of all ages, for three reasons:

1. The attributes of a cock: his comb, wattles, hooked beak, spurs, tail-feathers, ruffs on wings and neck, are so striking and universal that all children are familiar with them and are easily reminded of them by oral questioning.

2. The dramatic scene of combat, victory and defeat has so many pictorial features to capture a child's interest that it is gladly accepted as a painting theme.

3. The two-figure subject, unified within itself, leaves nothing to be desired. The oblong picture area may be used either horizontally or vertically, or even a square picture could be used equally well to excellent effect.

The requirements that a theme should be rooted in the visual experience of the pupils, sufficiently childlike in its content, and adapted to a child's artistic capacity are all satisfied by this subject. This being so, no further preparation for the task, such as the relation of a dramatic animal story about fighting cocks, the provision of visual stimulus perhaps in the shape of a living cock, is absolutely essential. It is therefore very interesting to compare the educational value of the work produced with and without the use of these additional stimuli.

Method

The difference is enormous. It is not a question, however, of greater activity or more varied treatment and it is not necessarily apparent in the results. Imperceptibly, however, the liveliness and visual stimulus of the lessons create a climate in which the children begin to feel in their element, because it has 'life' and 'generosity'. This generosity is founded upon a way of working with and for one another, in which self-recollection and absorbtion in the task predominate rather than bustle and frenzied activity. In this way something fundamental which can never be forgotten is nurtured.

Every artistic effort demands this genuine intensity of atmosphere if it is not to be a superficial waste of time. The material requirements for a task will be revealed in the particular pedagogic situation.

C 8   **Procession of Elephants (all ages)**

> According to age: modelling with clay (see *150 Techniques in Art*, p. 65). From 10 upwards, a paper relief masking the clay (see *150 Techniques in Art*, p. 74). Newspaper, wallpaper paste, powder colours.

A child is capable at all ages of expressing his artistic ideas in sculptural form. Although sculptured relief has deep roots in the history of art, it does not yield good results as a method of art teaching until the age of about 10. Our present theme is excellent for both the above techniques. It is a delightful subject for a group work in which each child produces a figure or relief of an elephant to join the procession. It is even more fun if the elephants are made to a scale so that each one can stand with its forelegs resting on the back of the preceding one.

Method

My own method might be a large figured relief at which groups of three or four children could work. The children learn the special technique of relief modelling experimentally. It can be a help to shape the rounded forms (trunk, legs) by rolling them and cutting the roll in half (knife or wire). Only large-figured reliefs can be masked with paper. The paper relief is begun with a layer of paper the size of the palm of the hand, which is applied with water only. The paper is first dipped in a bowl of water. Six to ten layers of paper dipped in wallpaper paste are next applied. To prevent blunting of the shapes, each layer must be pressed closely round the clay with the fingertips or a modelling tool. When it is absolutely dry the paper 'mask' can be lifted from the clay and painted in one or more colours.

Pair of Owls (all ages)   C 9

> Painting in poster colours. Drawing block, box of poster colours, brush.

Owls in a hole in the wall; a family of owls in the branches of a tree at night; owls flying about among the rafters—all these owl themes have qualities of both drama and mystery and a promising simplicity of form. A sitting owl, particularly at night, has an unbroken outline, a long or short upright oval. It is only upon closer inspection that one notices the pricks of two feather ears on its head. Its eyes, two perfect circles surrounded by wider circles of feathers, stare at one unseeingly like big wheels. At the base of the wide round head is the short hooked beak. The long wings lie close to the sides of the body; the short feathered legs with powerful claws grip the branch or stonework.

Method

The simple form of the owl's body suggests a direct painting technique. If a whole family of owls is to sit among the branches their arrangement in the picture must be planned when their perch is designed (Plate 8 a). Perhaps there is a whole gallery of owlets. The countless mysterious pairs of eyes cannot fail of their expressive effect. The plumage has a play of brownish, greenish blacks. A broad first coat of colour can be followed by detailed opaque painting of the varied plumage of the head, eyes, breast, wings and legs. The deep blue of the night sky makes a harmonious and effective background.

Further themes: Aquarium; Cats Playing with Tangled Skeins of Wool; A Dovecote; A Cage of Monkeys; A Caravan of Camels; The Lion's Den; Peacocks; Horses in a Paddock.

ARCHITECTURE

C 10 **Town on a River (10 upwards)**

> Painting in poster colours. Drawing block, pencil, box of poster colours, brush.

One of the best-known photographic views of London is from the south bank, across the Thames. This is because a river town is at its most 'photogenic' when it is seen from a distance, and the Thames with its bridges and boats provides the required decorative foreground. If 30 different photographers were to make studies of this view of London, 30 almost identical pictures would result. Thirty painters however would paint 30 different pictures full of individuality.

Together we can discuss the characteristics of such a view of a town with its towers and buildings, bridges and shipping. The 30 individual scenes which develop meanwhile in the visual imagination cannot yet be seen and compared. They are to be realised in our thirty characteristic pictures.

Method

It is best to begin a detailed picture such as this with a pencil drawing. By going round the class, the teacher can find out any problems or misunderstandings which need to be resolved. Many pupils need to be freed from formalism and may be helped by the encouragement to break away from rigidly conventional patterns. It is helpful to point out to the class any good composition produced by a classmate. The quality of a drawing can often be considerably enchanced by addition of the right details. The work of others may gain by being simplified to the basic forms. Themes like this one take a long time and therefore demand great perseverance. The more seriously the teacher takes his pupils' work, the more absorbed they will be in it. No one can possess greater zest for work than young people who sense that they are being rightly taught. Kindness

64

and encouragement educate the young to work conscientiously, never criticism and punishment.

Village Street (all ages)

> Large group work composed of separate paintings in poster colour. Drawing block, pencil, box of poster colours, brush, sheet of packing paper from large roll, powder colours, wallpaper paste, bristle or large flat brush, pins.

Children usually know their own house intimately. Now they are to put their knowledge to the test by drawing and painting it. In a class whose pupils all come from the same quarter of a town or from a small village, this task can be developed into a group picture representing the housing environment they know. For this task, combined planning is necessary if individual contributions are to fit in with one another to make the whole. A scale of measurement for the houses, the viewpoint from which they are to be shown and a generally accepted painting technique must be agreed upon.

Method

A street or crossroad is usually lined with houses on both sides. So it is possible for each child to draw his own house from the street side. Then, when they are put together, they can be placed side by side, vertically to the edges of the street in primitive symbolic arrangement, so that the street or intersection of streets seems to be seen from above in cross-section (Plate 8b). The individual cut-out paintings of the houses will have to be tried out in various arrangements for the whole composition before they are finally pasted down. Last of all, the picture will be enlivened with figures (people, vehicles, animals) which will again be tried in various positions before being added. The effect of the painting as class or hall decoration will depend upon its composition and can be considerably enhanced by a well-chosen background colour. Thr colour of the wrapping paper is too dull. Ordinary powder paint (a mixture of powder colour and gum arabic with water) is the cheapest and most vivid background medium.

The finished picture can be fixed to the wall with pins.

A Ruined Town (16 upwards)

> Pen and wash drawing. Pen-holder and drawing nib, drawing ink, box of water-colours, brush, white painting paper or block.

Our children still have before their eyes the towns which suffered from bombardment during the war. One day the last traces of destruction will disappear but it will take time. Their parents' reminiscences and graphic descriptions of scenes of destruction also linger in the children's minds.

To a painter's eye ruins have a sinister symbolism and also exciting paintable qualities. The weird sight of the bizarre remains of architecture once intact, standing against the sky, often grips even the young artist with uncanny power and stimulates his desire to paint.

Method

We will try to evoke this weird and terrible beauty in our drawings through the medium of the 'pen palette'. Ruins with their multiplicity of shapes and deformities are full of graphic detail; even the different textures of the walls and mouldering decorations are rich and varied subjects for the pen. Each ruined building is an individual figure, standing like a tombstone, blackened and weather-worn to tell of all the life that is past and play its part in the scene of dread. All the capacity of the imagination to create new pictorial worlds out of impressive experiences, all the power of artistic vision to synthesise disparate elements is here called into play. All realistic preoccupations can be set aside for we have entered the realm of dream and surreality.

A pen drawing is frequently heightened with a partial wash of delicate water colour. Naturally such a wash should be applied only if it can enhance the effect of the drawing. A pupil cannot judge in advance whether this is the case; it is advisable to try out the effect on a spare piece of paper.

Further themes: Skyscrapers; Gothic Cathedral; Modern Residential Suburb; Hill Village; Summer-house; Ruined Citadel; Building a New Church; Old Barns; Shopping Street; Indoor Swimming-Pool.

LANDSCAPE

Winter Landscape (10 upwards)

Painting in poster colours and gouache. Drawing block, box of poster colours, tube of white, sable brush.

Whereas younger children paint winter only through the seasonal happenings and activities which interest them, older ones gradually acquire the capacity to appreciate the winter scene as a background until eventually the snowy land itself, Nature in her winter mood, begins to interest them as an artistic theme. The same stages of development may be observed in their approach to all the seasons, in other words, to landscape itself.

There are therefore definite transitional stages and with one of them in mind we call our theme for 10-14-year-old pupils 'The Skating Pond in the Little Beech Wood' or 'The Toboggan Run in the Park' or 'A Ski Run in the Mountains'.

Method

Who could resist the idea of skating on the pond in the beech wood? (Plate 8c). It is not very large and holds very few skaters. The others are snow-balling, taking aim or hiding behind the tree-trunks. The great beeches stretch their bare branches to the wintry sky. To the young painter, the most important feature of the skating pond is its truly silver colour, and, of the trees, their burden of snow. For this reason we all agree, after general discussion, that we need tinted paper on which our white paint will show up well. The drawing block is too light, so we give it a coat of medium-toned grey-brown or grey-blue after preparing enough of the colour on our palettes (lid of paintbox). The forest floor too is snow-covered so that a new problem arises: as many of the children are using their paper horizontally, there is no way of distinguishing between earth and sky, no horizon in the picture. We decide therefore that, if the snow is to be painted on the topmost branches of the trees, it must not be painted on the ground up to the same height in the picture. We agree that the white of the snow is to fade away gradually towards the 'horizon'.

Windswept Avenue (14 upwards)

> Lino cut (see *150 Techniques in Art*, p. 57). Piece of lino, cutting
> tool, pane of glass, rubber roller, printing ink, absorbent paper,
> old newspaper.

The aim of our lino cut is to render the strong theme of movement as expressively as possible.

The wind rushes down an avenue of poplars, bending the
leafless treetops as it passes. A few tardy pedestrians press on-
ward, their coats whipped back by the night storm.

The more limited the subject, the more varied its demands
on the imagination. Expressive line is never formless; hasty
frenzied execution is only apparently demanded by such a
wild scene. There are moreover various possibilities of treatment, so that careful planning is needed. We shall need to try
different kinds of design. Each fresh design should either im-
prove on the previous one or develop an entirely new idea. We
shall discover by genuine concentration, each upon our own
design, how diversely such a theme can be treated.

Method

Many older pupils are inhibited in the drawing of the human
figure by self-criticism because they do not feel their figures to
be natural enough. This theme allows the human figure to be
represented in a highly simplified form, enveloped in a coat,
the head almost hidden. There is no question of any detail
(e.g. facial features). As an aid to the proportioning of the
figures, a pupil may act as model. He will show how the limbs
are balanced, the head bent, the body pressed forward in walking against the wind. At this stage the representation of trees
might also be studied afresh through direct observation. The
branches spring from the trunk, the twigs from the branches
and therefore may not be added on at will. The part is to the
whole as our own arms are to our bodies. All the branches of a
tree follow the general direction of its growth. Every kind of
tree has its own particular rhythm of growth, which determines its lines from trunk to twig and distinguishes it from
every other tree. This theme favours a white-line cut as the
black background (night) would then predominate.

Painting in wax crayons, poster colours or powder paints; also as
a fresco in poster- or powder colours (see *150 Techniques in Art*,
p. 28). Drawing block, sable or bristle brush.

The youngest children may illustrate freely. For the middle
and upper classes a limitation of this, in itself almost boundless,
theme is advisable. If the paper is used horizontally, there is
room for two large apple trees. Many adjuncts are needed for
apple-picking: ladders, baskets, and a cart to carry away the
fruit. Boys and girls are picking and sorting. Some little boys
are snatching the chance to climb the trees. The picture is full
of movement and gaiety.

Method

The trees can either be treated analytically, as structures—
trunk, branches, twigs, leaves, all clearly related and defined—
or as masses, so that an outspread branch becomes a complex
of foliage. Both styles come naturally to children and both can
be developed, but experience has taught that a tree, treated
as a mass and painted without good guidance from the teacher,
readily degenerates into either a big green lollipop on a stick
or a mere haze of 'may-be' (pseudo-impressionism). For this
reason many teachers prefer the 'structural' tree. For the
present theme it is certainly preferable as it is more 'transparent', can be climbed, and allows decisive drawing of every
detail.

The representation of the human figure also tempts the
weaker members of the class to schematic treatment. The
remedy is a theme involving movement. Climbing boys demand
ever-renewed experiment in the drawing of movement and
schematic formulae have to be abandoned.

Children always start with the objects in the picture when
they paint. Sky and earth are not objects to the child's way of
thinking. If he has to paint the sky afterwards, he may easily
spoil that part of his picture which was painted with spontaneous interest, i.e. the detailed objects. For this reason we
either renounce colouring the sky altogether or cover the paper
with background colour before detailed painting begins.

Further themes: Volcanic Eruption; Winding Road on the
Wooded Mountainside; Willows in the Mist; Moonlit Trees;

Dying Trees on the Marsh;   Woodlands in Autumn;   Seaside Creek;   Stormclouds over the Sea;   Forest Path between Tall Pines and Firs;   Landscape with Rainbow.

II THEMES OF FREE IMAGINATION

D HISTORICAL TRADITION

OLD TESTAMENT

Daniel in the Lion's Den (all ages)   D 1

> Painting in poster colours; also as group work in powder colours
> on large sheet of packing paper. Drawing block, pencil, box of
> poster colours; or sheet of packing paper from a roll, 68 × 40 inches,
> powder colours, gum arabic or other base, bristle brush.

The Old Testament contains an inexhaustible store of pictures.
The impressions that children store up in their Bible classes
are so rich and varied that art classes should often be linked
with current religious instruction. What subject could be more
dramatic than the miraculous and profound stories of Daniel
and Nebuchadnezar, and particularly the outstanding description in the Sixth Book of Daniel of the preservation of the
prophet in the lions' den. It is not easy to find out what gives
a child his initial impulse to make a picture, whether it is the
sheer pleasure of the activity itself or the feeling of being inspired by some outside event which seeks expression in art.
Which of the two experiences is primary, which the means and
which the end cannot easily be ascertained. We accept the rule
of 'the primary need for interest in the subject-matter' as
applicable at least to primary classes, with the implication that
a specific interest in the form develops only gradually (from
10 onwards). This axiom takes no account, however, of the
equally primary urge towards manual artistic expression. We
must assume that these two primary interests flow together
almost indivisibly. With this idea in mind, we always choose
themes which will appeal to them simultaneously.

Method

It is easy to preceive that, apart from the quality of its subject-
matter, the lions' den theme possesses formal pictorial qualities
which are the more potent, the closer our picture is to the
centre of the action, i.e. the den, and the more narrowly the
figures are confined within them both. The den should be
scarcely big enough for Daniel and his lions. Next the question

71

arises whether our visual memory of a lion is clear enough for us to draw a whole den full of them. It is possible that many of the children have never set eyes on a lion, or that, even if they have seen one in a circus, a zoo, or a film, no clear impression has remained.

Here we touch upon one of the fundamentals of art teaching, which bears not only upon the question of the visual concept of a lion but upon the problem of the concept itself in general and of how far it must be based upon direct visual experience. We are nowadays aware that a visual concept can be acquired not only through the observation of nature but also through an imaginative stimulus, that is to say, through graphic verbal description, and also that it makes no difference to the quality of the artistic representation whether the initial concept sprang from observation of nature or from the arbitrary world of phantasy.

D 2　**The Animals entering Noah's Ark (all ages)**

> Large mural stencil print in bronze on a black ground, group work (see *150 Techniques in Art,* p. 57). Drawing block, pencil, scissors, packing paper painted with black powder paint—powder paint and gum arabic—or bought black paper, bronze powder paint, bristle brush.

In the story of the Flood we are told that Noah, at God's command, led into the Ark one male and one female of every animal. Why not let the children in the class choose partners, each couple to produce a pair of animals and to cut out their drawings to make the stencils for our large group picture? The elephants should be as large as the block permits, the cock and hen a little smaller (not in their actual proportionate sizes, but all the animals fairly large).

Method

A large sheet of packing paper is painted black with powder paint and laid on two joined tables for the background. As they are completed, the cut-out animals join the procession which winds towards the Ark (which will have to be a separate task) (Plate 9a). All the figures can still be moved about into experimental arrangements. When the best has been found, we mark the positions of the animals with little signs and numbers and put the figures on one side. Now begins the process of

72

stencilling. With the bristle brush the bronze colour (powder and a base, e.g. varnish) is painted, working outwards, over the edges of each stencil laid in its marked position on the background. When the stencil is removed we find a black picture of the animal surrounded by an aura of bronze. If the animals are close enough together, their auras touch and this helps the unity of the composition. We take pains to achieve density of composition; we keep the figures a certain distance from the edges of the background, thus a print-like unity to the centre of the picture. This black border is a frame for the finished picture.

Building the Tower of Babel (all ages) D 3

Silhouette, group work. Scissors, paintbrush, paste, ordinary white paper, so-called 'scrap' paper is best, two sheets of black book-covering paper, 6 pins.

The technique determines the treatment of the building, which is white on a black ground, in the immediate foreground, animated by the many figures of the builders. Ladders, planks and workers are its elements. The length and breadth of the sheets of paper is agreed and cut out. Their size depends upon that of the tower which itself is determined by the background. Two sheets of black book-covering paper are gummed together side by side so that their length is used vertically. Proportions may be guessed.

Method

After an introductory discussion of the meaning of the story of the Tower of Babel, and combined planning of the work as suggested in the foregoing notes, each child starts by cutting out a ladder and a plank. The cut-outs are then given a coat of paste with the bristle brushes over sheets of newspaper. They are left to soak up the paste and, if necessary a second coat is applied. The background should preferably be pinned to the wall with 4-6 pins. The building of the tower can begin when the first cut-outs are ready, the ladders being placed some distance from the lower edge of the picture, mainly in perpendicular positions, the planks next as landings and platforms, mainly horizontally (Plate 10a). Exceptions such as slanting or horizontal ladders, diagonally supporting planks, etc., may be added at the children's suggestion or according to the requirements of the composition. We avoid rigid uniformity of arrangement in favour of a freely rhythmic growth of the composition. The tower-like effect will be increased if the scaffolding gets narrower towards the top. The pasting on is easier if the pressing down is done with a wad of newspaper. Children who have finished their first task can take the sheets already cut to the correct size for the builders, cut out the figures in working attitudes, and paste them in suitable positions. We aim at a lively grouping of the figures.

Further themes: Creation of the Animals; Adam and Eve in Paradise; Cain Slaying Abel; Abraham Sacrificing Isaac; Jacob Wrestling with the Angel; The Dove bringing Noah the Olive Branch; The Dance round the Golden Calf; The Trumpets of Jericho; David Playing the Harp before Saul; Jonah in the Whale's Belly.

NEW TESTAMENT

D 4   **The Flight into Egypt (all ages)**

Painting in poster colours (also in powder or designer's colours) on tinted paper (packing paper, wallpaper, etc.) with bristle brush (round e.g. No. 9 or 12; also with sable brush on usual drawing block); initial drawing in charcoal (or pencil).

The larger the sheet of paper, the greater the freedom achieved in drawing with charcoal and painting with a large brush. If white paper is used as background, only one colour effect is possible which is darker than the background itself; a tinted background permits contrast of light and shade. This enrichment of the medium allows self-expression and experiment in colour and should be used at every opportunity. Winter subjects such as this, with snowflakes and snow on the branches, are hard to tackle without tinted paper.

Method

The story of the flight into Egypt is told in St Matthew's Gospel. We forego a wide landscape background and concentrate on the depiction of the flight as a simple group of large figures. Mary rides with the child on the ass which Joseph is leading. Palms or other exotic trees and bushes may complete the picture (Plate 9b). The unity of the composition is the most

74

Plate 7

b Cockfight (C7), in poster colours, by a 12-year-old boy.
Height 24 inches

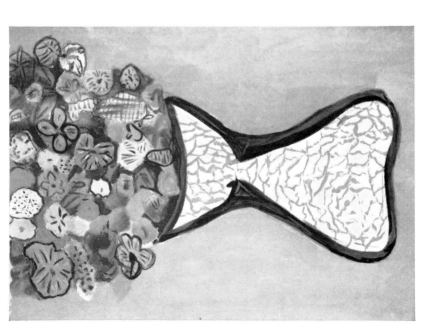

a Vase of Flowers (C4), in poster colours, by a 12-year-old
girl. Height 24 inches

Plate 8

a Pair of Owls (C9), in powder colours, by a student teacher. Width 24 inches

b Village Street (C 11), appliqué of paintings, by the top form of a country school. Width 60 inches

c Winter Landscape (C 13), gouache, by a 13-year-old boy. Width 24 inches

Plate III

Still Life (C1-3), sand painting, by a 17-year-old girl. Width 20 inches

important thing. The children are familiar with the subject; no fresh stimulus to the imagination through external impressions is necessary. Their task is to represent an already existing individual conception of the scene as clearly and exactly as possible. The teacher will not demand a naturalistic drawing but rather that every line should express a clear personal image of the subject. This aim of clarity may be furthered if the charcoal drawing is followed by a definitive dark brush drawing. The inner areas are then completely covered with thick poster colour. This method of painting follows in essentials that of all early periods of art. (Among Giotto's fresco paintings in the Arena Chapel at Padua there is a particularly beautiful version of the Flight into Egypt which a child could appreciate.)

The Calming of the Storm (all ages)   D 5

> Painting in poster colours. Drawing block, pencil, box of poster colours, brush.

St Matthew relates the background story of the stilling of the tempest with stark simplicity. In so few lines, the dramatic event could not be more graphically described. With every sentence a picture is set before us. Everything is present and near to us. Our picture must make the story present and near once more.

Method

The paper is used vertically, so that the little boat, filling its whole width, appears cramped and helpless, especially if the figures of its crew are comparatively large and close to one another. Tossed by the wild waves, the boat heels dangerously and lies at an angle to the side of the picture. The mast points steeply downwards, dragged by the torn sail. The wild gestures of the crew, crowded into the narrow vessel, reveal their growing fear of disaster. The only one who sleeps is the one who can save them. A preliminary drawing will clarify the construction of the picture. The wildness of the waves can be drawn, not by wild scribbling but by great breakers, separately drawn, with troughs, peaks and foaming crests, or by rollers breaking against one another, each of which is clearly distinguished by the parallel curves of its development. The movement of the wind and storm clouds can similarly be shown in the drawing.

To heighten the effect of a drawing so full of movement with colour is no easy task. The whole effect can easily be lost in a washy mess if the task is not divided up into planned sections, to be completed with care and concentration, and if the excitement of the theme itself is allowed to tempt us into slapdash, impetuous painting.

The generous use of white and black helps to heighten the colour by the contrast of light and dark passages and avoids both a monotonous stew of mixed medium tones and the alternative clash of raw colours.

D 6 The Last Supper (12 upwards)

Mural-size painting in poster colours, group work. Drawing block, 22 × 18 inches, or loose sheet, pencil, box of poster colours, brush, scissors, grey wrapping paper 40 × 66 inches, wallpaper paste, old newspaper.

We imagine a long table at the centre of which Jesus sits with six of the apostles on either side, to right and left, just as in Leonardo's great painting of the Last Supper (to give a deeper understanding of which this theme was partly chosen). The composition is to be assembled from separately made figures, each drawn and painted by one pupil at his own drawing board. We agree that the figures are to fill the whole paper used vertically, so that there need be no measuring the proportions. Horizontally, through the exact centre of the sheet, is drawn the upper (further) edge of the table; the lower edge may be 1-2 inches lower. The thickness of the table is indicated by a line about half-an-inch lower still. Ten apostles and the figure of Jesus are pictured seated behind the table, the other two apostles at each end in profile. Food and drink is laid out on the table.

Method

All the children in the class work on this picture simultaneously. Since their number does not coincide with that of the figures, a suitable solution is found. The more advanced pupils, who have earned the right to be trusted to use their own judgment (the aim of education), decide which figures are most suitable for inclusion in the final picture. In classes of younger children it may be better to let more than one picture be composed. Alternatively remaining figures may be kept for some other purpose.

This noble theme demands the greatest sincerity. Who can hope to depict Jesus, John, Peter, Judas? The hands and gestures, expressions and attitudes should all express their spiritual communion. The older pupils may practise drawing real drapery before attempting the garments. They should then draw from imagination to achieve the simplest and most unified effect. Modern dress would be possible.

The cut-out figures are arranged as close together as possible. Parts which are hidden by overlapping and therefore superfluous can be cut off (e.g. parts of the table). The positions are then marked on the background (grey packing paper), and the parts of the picture pasted on and pressed down with newspaper. For further additions to the background (details of the room, etc.) a drawing (e.g. brush and ink) will suffice.

Further themes: The Annunciation; Adoration of the Magi; Baptism of Christ; Miraculous Draught of Fishes; Return of the Prodigal Son; Entry into Jerusalem; Jesus Carrying the Cross; Jesus Rising from the Dead; Angel Releasing Peter from Prison.

LEGENDS

Madonna in the Temple (12 upwards)   D 7

> Painting in poster colours. Drawing block, possibly 22 × 18 inches, pencil, box of poster colours, brush.

Our educational aim is to induce a deeper understanding of one of the later mediaeval paintings of the Madonna, van Eyck's Madonna in the Temple. The method of setting the pupils the same theme is especially appropriate in this case. The child is to encounter the same problems which the master solved and to tackle them in his own way. A real wish to look at the masterpiece and the capacity to appreciate it are developed at the same time.

Method

The theme is introduced by a description of the colours and forms of van Eyck's painting, but no reproduction of it is shown. The description may be detailed or may be generalised to leave greater freedom to the imagination. It is important that the size of the figures in relation to the whole should be such that the subject is not lost amid the background detail. When the size has been agreed, the upper and lower limits of the figures or the length and position of the heads can, if necessary, be marked by faint horizontal lines.

The privilege of painting a Madonna and the prospect of seeing in its full splendour a reproduction of the famous masterpiece, which has been described to them, should be sufficient inducements to the children to try to paint the most beautiful picture they can (Plate 10 b).

During the preliminary drawing, the teacher divides the task into successive parts, in order to help his pupils to concentrate on the chief parts of their picture. The first task may be to make a careful pencil drawing of the Madonna; the second, to draw her throne with all its decoration, and so on. The pupil organises his work either independently or with the teacher's timely guidance. Not until the whole picture has been lovingly drawn can painting begin; this too must be planned for concentration on the essential stages. The teacher should leave decisions about the drawing of the picture and the colour almost entirely to the pupils, demanding only that they preserve a clear line in every detail of the drawing, choose harmonious colours which distinguish the objects and their various parts from one another, and keep the outlines of the areas of colour clear and distinct. This last is a matter of good brushwork which comes with practice. The theme allows elaborate decorations. The parts to be decorated must receive their background colours before the decoration is applied. On a light background the decoration must be darker, on a dark one, lighter.

D 8   St Michael and the Dragon (all ages)

> Paper mosaic (see *150 Techniques in Art*, p. 45). Drawing block, pencil, box of poster colours, brush, scissors, large sheet of packing paper, wallpaper paste, old newspaper.

The combat of Michael the Archangel with the Dragon, like the legend of St George who fought on horseback with the Devil in the shape of a dragon, is a theme suited to the young in many ways. Its gripping drama and profound symbolism invariably appeal to all age-groups. This wonderful theme has motivated many painters from Raphael to Barlach; today it is

Plate 9

a   Animals Leaving Noah's Ark (D2), stencil, by a student group. Width 80 inches

b   The Flight into Egypt (D4), in powder colours, by a 10-year-old girl. Width 40 inches

Plate 10

*a The Tower of Babel (D3), silhouette appliqué,
by a kindergarten group. Height 80 inches*

*b Madonna in the Temple (D7),
in poster colours, by an 11-year-
old boy. Height 26 inches*

*c Laocöon (D 10), in poster colours,
by a 14-year-old boy. Width 24 inches*

the turn of the children and adolescents to depict the longed-for triumph of goodness over the evil one, the serpent.

Method

To start the large group work in paper mosaic, we set all members of the class the competitive task of producing the design best suited to the subject and medium. The winner is decided by vote. He draws a large charcoal version on the wrapping paper (free hand, not by mechanical means). Meanwhile the rest of the class paint sheets from the block in the various colours suitable for a mosaic. Five paint in brown, five in green or blue tones. We also need black for the outlines and a little carmine or vermilion for the dragon's mouth. The size of the little 'tiles' is agreed (about one square inch) and the sheets are then cut up into little squares. Each colour is put into a separate box. Now the pasting on of the tiles can begin, preferably with the outlines and inner lines of the figures, which will provide a sort of framework for the building of the picture. We are careful to keep to a regular width ($1/8$ inch) and cut the tiles where necessary to follow the outlines of the figures, so that uniformity is preserved. The finished picture can be attached to the wall with a few pins.

Saint Francis Preaching to the Birds (all ages)   D 9

> Painting in poster colours. Drawing block, pencil, box of poster paints, brush.

The legends about St Francis of Assisi tell us of the admirable simplicity and loving kindness of this man, devoted servant of God. He told even the fishes and the birds of God's greatness and of His love for them. Such legendary incidents of his life inspire us to a similar simplicity and reverence. We perceive again the double role of art teaching which is not only subject to its own laws and specific means for the education of a human being as artist, but at the same time to the parallel demands of his development as a human being, which it can further and serve, since they do not conflict with its own aims. In order to integrate these two tasks, the art teacher must choose subjects whose spiritual content and significance transcend the sphere of art and focus them so that they 'become pictures' and can be fruitful for art teaching. It is in this sense that we have 'focused' our present theme.

Method

Using our paper either vertically or horizontally (or using a square sheet), we can depict the saint standing, half-kneeling or seated, his head and gestures directed towards the birds, which have settled in front of him or flutter around him and which complete the composition. Very diverse compositions are possible, according to the proportion of the central figure to the picture space and the close or loose grouping of the birds. Trees might also be used as perches for the feathered congregation.

A careful drawing will be followed by an equally careful painting. The background will either be coloured beforehand (as sky, grass), or be left plain. Subsequent painting of the background colour between fluttering birds or branches is very laborious; it is difficult to keep an even tone and to avoid a blotchy effect and smudged outlines.

Pupils who have tackled this theme themselves are capable of looking at Giotto's famous Saint Francis and the Birds with new awareness.

Further themes: St Christopher; Saint Martin on Horseback Sharing his Coat with the Beggar; St Francis Preaching to the Fishes; St Jerome and the Lion; Temptation of St Anthony (subject of the Isenheim Altarpiece); St George and the Dragon; A Concert of Angels (*cf.* van Eyck and Grünewald); St Eustace and the Hart (*cf.* Dürer's engraving).

MYTHS

D 10 **Laocöon (12 upwards)**

Several techniques: painting in poster colours after pencil drawing or large paper-relief on clay (or oil clay), etc. (see *150 Techniques in Art*, p. 74). For the latter: newspaper, wallpaper paste, clay or oil clay (various modelling materials); for the base: pane of glass, plastic cloth, lino, etc.

The world of myth contains an immeasurable wealth of dramatic themes. Great painters and sculptors have given artistic form to many mythological themes such as the story of Laocöon from the Greek saga of the Trojan war. Laocöon, the Trojan priest who had warned his fellow-citizens against the cunning gift of the Greeks (the Trojan Horse), is strangled, together with his two sons, by avenging snakes sent by the Gods. The artist always chooses themes which are pictorial. This means, in terms of art education, that the theme set to the pupil must fulfil not only the obvious requirement that it be childlike but must also be intrinsically pictorial. The Laocöon theme is so to a high degree. The rhythmic movements of the figures and the winding forms of the snakes make a well unified composition whether the picture area is used vertically or horizontally.

Method

We begin with a dramatic account of the myth. There is no doubt of the pictorial and dramatic crux of the story. A graphic description will easily evoke a vivid mental image of the figures in combat with the powerful snakes coiling and encircling them, for all pictorial subjects may be regarded as already known to the imagination; no further stimulus from external visual experience will be needed. It is actually better to let the pupils draw straight from individual imagination without attempting to enact such scenes, lest the spontaneous growth of the picture from the pictorial image be interrupted by intervening impressions.

A theme involving wrestling and fighting holds especial interest for boys. This interest can be brought into play by pointing out how the fear and desperate exertion of the men can be expressed in their staring eyes, dishevelled hair and wild gestures (Plate 10c). We may also point out that the winding of the snakes around the struggling bodies is a vehement lashing movement on which the fusion of the whole composition at the centre of the combat depends. In this way enthusiasm for the subject-matter can be translated into concentration upon the compositional unity.

When everyone has looked at the pictures produced by the class, they may be shown the Hellenistic Laocöon group. Only then is the full capacity for its appreciation present.

The Fall of Icarus (8 upwards) D 11

> Underglass painting (see *150 Techniques in Art,* p. 83). Pane of glass, box of poster colours, brush, coloured paper, gummed strips, scissors.

The moving events of the Greek myth of Daedalus and Icarus have inspired extremely diverse works of which Breughel's painting is perhaps the strangest.

As they come near to the sun the waxen wings melt and Icarus plunges into the sea.

It would be a splendid introduction to the theme, if the teacher were to tell the story so vividly that the children themselves relived the unforeseen and terrifying moment in which Icarus feels himself no longer borne by wings and turns his eyes, till now fixed upon the sun, to the abyss into which he is already falling. This impression would concentrate their visual imagination on the falling figure, the pictorial centre of the theme.

Method

Each pupil has a reasonably large piece of glass (remainders from a glazier cut into rectangles) in front of him. On a piece of paper of the same dimensions he draws a well composed design: Icarus falling, head and body already turned downwards, arms vainly seeking support from the already broken wings, fills the whole picture. The free movements of the limbs and the size of the wings help to balance the masses in the composition. The finished drawing is laid under the glass and now begins the painting in really thick poster colour on what will eventually be the back of the glass. We shall paint only the naked body of the falling boy as an area; the pinions of the great wings, which fill a large proportion of the picture, will be drawn with the brush in detail, the outlines, quill and (if possible) the tiny hairs of each feather being carefully elaborated. Between the lines of the brush drawing, the transparent glass is left as a background. When the colour is dry, we lay a suitably coloured piece of paper (blue, red, gold, etc.) on the painted side. From the other side of the glass, the right side, we can judge of the effect. A gummed strip binds the edge of the glass and holds the protective paper background in place.

D 12 The Trojan Horse (10 upwards)

Painting in poster colours. Drawing block, box of poster paints, brush.

The soul of a great people flowed into the imagery of Greek myths. Prometheus, Hercules, Oedipus, Achilles and Odysseus are the mythical heroes of ancient Hellas and the sons of the Gods. The mythical inhabitants of the earth and the under-world are giants and cyclops, lapiths and centaurs, sirens and shades. Troy and Thebes, Athens and Sparta, were the famous cities of heroic and tragic destiny.

Our theme seems immortal for it still stirs the imaginations of the young after many centuries. It is also essentially pic-torial. Into the fantastic architectural scene of a city of ancient saga is introduced the fantastic implement of a fantastic event, the gigantic wooden horse, within whose belly the heroes are hiding, ready to spring out that night and overthrow Troy by their cunning.

Method

The elaborate form and content of narrative themes make great demands on the perseverance of pupils. The children with the most enthusiasm for the subject often take longest to commit their wealth of ideas to paper. If we consider only the architectural possibilities that our subject offers to the im-agination, we are at once faced with the question: how long should such a task be allowed to take, and what means can be found to maintain the pupil's pleasure in it? The first thing we must realise is that the conscientiousness and powers of perseverance of the pupils are directly dependent on the general working atmosphere during the lessons, that is to say, entirely dependent upon the spirit created by the teacher's own attitude to the work. Experience also shows that the young are capable of great feats of perseverance and of constantly renewed zest and pleasure in activity. We are even convinced that the de-mand for such effort is a fulfilment of one of their deepest desires, however appearances may seem to belie us. Many of the pictures reproduced in this book took the pupils two or more months in which they had two art classes a week. Con-trolled stages of work are helpful in that they prevent the prospect of final achievement being lost through impatient, hasty work. Controlled divisions of the task must be set not only for the drawing but also for the sequence of the painting.

Further themes: Polyphemus; Hercules and the Lion; Battle of the Lapiths and Centaurs; Pegasus; The Castle of the Holy Grails.

HISTORY

D 13 Charlemagne Enthroned (10 upwards)

> Foil relief (see *150 Techniques in Art,* p. 74). Embossed line technique: aluminium or copper foil and special tool can be bought from art suppliers, but blunt pencil, hardwood modelling tool, etc. will do. Drawing ink, glass-paper, paint-brush, newspaper.

Subjects taken from history need not be statements of historical fact but should rather be imaginatively and symbolically true. Furthermore, by no means all historical events can be represented pictorially; for instance 'The Union of England and Scotland' cannot be compared as a pictorial theme with the 'Great Fire of London'. In our choice of historical themes we must still seek above all the childlike and the intrinsically pictorial.

Method

These basic demands are fulfilled by the theme 'Charlemagne Enthroned'. Here it is not a question of painting the portrait of a man about whose appearance nothing definite is known, but of the free play of imagination. The limitation of the theme to one figure allows the imagination to concentrate on the regal splendour of the figure wearing the crown and coronation robe and seated upon his magnificent throne.

The work begins with a pencil drawing to the measurements of the foil sheet. Its transference to the foil is easy if the latter is laid on a hard surface and the lines of the pencil drawing which is laid over it are lightly impressed. The actual relief process follows; it consists of deep graving of the lines with the hard blunt tool, the foil being laid on thick resilient layers of smooth newspaper, so that a soft impression is given. The underside is the right side. Its raised lines and possibly also some embossed areas can be further accentuated if the whole picture is blackened (drawing ink) and the raised portions finally polished with sand-paper.

D 14 Tournament (10 upwards)

> Painting in poster colours. Drawing block, pencil, box of poster colours, brush.

This theme, limited to two knights whose figures fill the picture area (used horizontally) allows the full panoply of a child's idea of pictorial splendour to be unfolded. A graphic description introduces the theme. The gleaming weapons, the armour of the men and horses, the rich bridles, beautifully decorated shields and saddle-cloths, and finally the noble movements of the prancing horses as the combatants close in upon one another make one self-contained picture. The fortress in the background, the meadow gay with flowers round off the whole, unless a plain gold ground like that of an icon is preferred.

Method

The limitation of the composition to two combatants at close quarters filling the picture horizontally does not deny the child the possibility of individual creative expression (Plate II). This is proved not only by the fact that no picture produced is quite like any other but above all by the evidence that even the most talented pupil can use all his capacities. At the same time this limitation allows even the less gifted to give a good account of themselves, the test of a good theme. It is certainly best if a whole exhibition of pictures can result from a theme which the whole class has understood and planned together; it is equally certain that the strong and genuine desire of certain pupils to create a picture in another way should not be denied.

Visit to a Monument (10 upwards)   D 15

> Large brush drawing painted afterwards in poster colours in a limited range of colours. Drawing block 22 × 18 inches if possible, or loose sheet, box of poster colours, sable or possibly bristle brush.

A theme like this renders an historical subject pictorial. In a sense, it renders it doubly so, since one artist, in this case a sculptor, has already treated it. The idea for our picture, however, goes a little beyond history into the realm of fantasy, for we are going to invent the existence of the monument we are depicting and to dedicate it to some historical personage who has none as far as we know but deserves one. Perhaps it will be Alexander the Great or Paul the Apostle—or even the art teacher! We shall lend reality to our invented monument by showing some people looking at it; why shouldn't we be the spectators ourselves?

Method

Only a skillful teacher, gifted with warm-hearted humour, can hope to bring off this venture into a theme which is both humorous and 'eccentric', so that his pupils have fun with it and still work in earnest. Of course we could just as well visit and draw a real monument nearby, the equestrian statue of some former ruler of the district perhaps. The first stage of the task is a bold uncorrectable brush drawing in ink or dark poster colour. It is easy to foresee that it may be best to begin by representing the bystanders before the monument itself. They need not be full-length figures. It may help the composition if half-length figures, or even heads only, surround the lower edge of the picture. The chief figure on his pedestal is then added in suitable proportion. The remaining areas in the composition can be filled by trees in the park, etc. The dark brush drawing is to remain visible as the framework of the finished picture. The inner areas painted with a palette restricted to shades of one colour (e.g. blue) which are graded by admixture of black or white.

Further themes: Nero Fiddles while Rome Burns; Murder of a Tyrant; Destruction of Pompeii; Coronation of Henry VIII; Le Roi Soleil.

Plate 11

Tournament (D14), in poster colours, by an 11-year-old boy. Width 24 inches

Plate 12

*a The Fisherman and his
Wife (E1), in poster col-
ours, by a 12-year-old girl.
Width 21 inches*

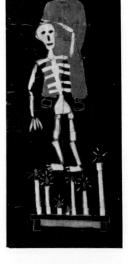

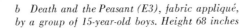

*b Death and the Peasant (E3), fabric appliqué,
by a group of 15-year-old boys. Height 68 inches*

*c Vobis and Tehuan (E4), paper
and foil appliqué, by a class.
Height 64 inches*

E FAIRY TALE AND ADVENTURE

FOLK TALES

The Fisherman and his Wife (all ages)

E 1

> Painting in poster colours. Drawing block, pencil, box of poster colours, brush.

In the middle classes many children have a tendency to imitate fashionable formulae. The faces, clothing, hair and physical proportions of girls and young women, princesses and fairies are in especial danger of becoming sentimental clichés. Diversion to other subjects is the best cure. Witches, unlike fairy tale princesses, are immune from the danger of being turned into fashion models. We also avoid all stories about sweet little dwarfs, toad-stool houses and young deer, which lead to imitations of mass-produced garden gnomes and of deer with big eyes like Bambi. Our treasure-house of folk tales offers innumerable hardier and more full-blooded subjects which allow of forceful and spontaneous interpretation.

Method

The story of the Fisherman and his Wife is one of these strong, racy and at the same time childishly magical themes. The pictorial climax comes immediately before the climax of the narrative. All the insatiable ambitions of the fisherman's wife have been fulfilled one after another. She has become Pope and lives in a palace. But her ambition will not leave her in peace: now she wants to become Almighty God. So her obedient husband goes once again unwillingly to the 'little flounder in the sea' to tell it of his wife's wish. This, the culminating point of the story, evokes our picture: the scene, the sea-shore with the fish and the fisherman and, at a distance, the wife as the Pope in front of her palace (Plate 12 a).

Younger pupils can be left to illustrate the story spontaneously. From the age of ten onwards, the task becomes more and more a question of arranging the figures and objects into a well-composed picture, of relating the colour masses into a well balanced unity. A not too detailed composition sketch is followed by painting in strong poster colours to cover the entire picture. The naive instinct for colour shown by young children must gradually be replaced by the planned colour composition to be achieved by the seniors.

E 2 The Witch from Jorinde and Joringel (all ages)

Direct painting in poster colours. Drawing block, box of poster colours, brush.

This fairy tale is one of the most beautiful and moving preserved for us by the Brothers Grimm. Like nearly all fairy tales, it contains many scenes which are highly suitable for illustration. Often individual figures and objects can be depicted in isolation and make excellent themes for a large single-figure composition, as for instance the figure of the witch hiding in a bush and holding in her hand Jorinde, whom she has transformed into a little bird.

Method

Direct painting means uncorrectable painting. The advantage of this treatment is its loosening effect. Children who are inhibited in their drawing and who constantly rub out what they have done, are persuaded indirectly through this technique and medium, to accept and appreciate their own work. The obvious disadvantage of the method, namely that less detail can be expressed in it, can be overcome by subsequent brush drawing of the structural detail of the larger areas (e.g. the bush, foliage of the tree) with thicker paint. In general, full use should be made of the opportunity afforded by poster colours (and also by ordinary powder with a size base) for elaboration by painting light on dark and dark on light. Essential corrections can be made in this way.

E 3 Death and the Peasant (14 upwards)

Fabric appliqué on wrapping paper (see *150 Techniques in Art*, p. 52). Paper for designing, pencil, sheet of packing paper, remains of fabric, scissors, wallpaper paste, bristle or large flat brush, charcoal, drawing ink.

Large single figures are most suitable for translation into this kind of appliqué. Our subject will be symbolised by the figures of the peasant and of Death and by a series of burned candle ends of various lengths. Various juxtapositions of the figures are possible as well as variety of pose and gesture (Plate 12b).

Method

Each pupil sketches a composition from the elements described to him. The most suitable design is drawn large in charcoal on the sheet of wrapping paper. A brush and ink line over the charcoal fixes the drawing. We make the picture with scraps of thin material chosen and cut out to fit into the areas left by the lines of the drawing. A good coat of wallpaper paste holds the fabric to the paper. The ink drawing may (but need not) remain visible. The background, as a foil to the figures, is covered with a suitable powder colour. To cover it with fabric is advisable only if this would not detract from the sharpness of the figures.

Further themes: The Goose-Girl; Ali Baba Finding the Treasure; Hänsel and Gretel; The Seven Swans; The Golden Goose.

MODERN FAIRY TALES

Vobis and Tehuan (all ages)   E 4

Ragged paper appliqué. Drawing block, coloured paper, adhesive.

Vobis, the Chief's daughter, who has been transformed into a gigantic bird of prey, is freed from the spell by Tehuan, the Chief's son. To free her, he must risk his life by letting her pursue him under the At tree, where he is at the mercy of the bird being unarmed. But the At tree lowers its branches to embrace them both. Thus it frees Vobis from the spell and, as she sheds her feathers, they fall upon Tehuan, and he receives the full dress of a chieftain.

We take these two splendid feathered figures from the Mexican children's story, Vobis as the great bird and Tehuan in his Chief's dress as the subjects of our picture (Plate 12c). Half the class chooses to create one figure, half the other. Finally the figures are suitably paired off to form small combined pictures.

Method

For our ragged paper appliqué, we choose any coloured paper except the variety which is sold ready gummed: old decorative paper, present wrapping paper, or paper we have coloured ourselves and which has not the repellent gloss and strident colour usual in bought coloured paper. The background is a sheet of our drawing block or a piece of old newspaper. We try out the technique to get in practice. It was deliberately chosen for the theme of feathered figures, since it is quite natural to build up the figures gradually by 'dressing' them with rags of paper for their feathers and clothing. A preliminary design is not essential: the figures should grow from feather to feather until they are complete.

Each finished appliqué is then torn away from its temporary background and remounted with its companion figure (preferably against a dark background).

E 5   **The Fairy Coach from 'Ta and Ani' (all ages)**

> Wax-engraving (see *150 Techniques in Art*, p. 57). Drawing block, wax crayons, waterproof ink or designer's colour, bristle or large flat brush, engraving tool (i.e. penknife, nail-file, etc.).

It is not always easy or even possible to find stories which supply lively and the same time childlike themes to suit the teacher's particular educational purpose. It is therefore occasionally advisable to invent one's own fairy tale. 'Ta and Ani' was one such homemade tale.

I first had the visual image of a fairy coach in which a fairy tale king was driving, drawn by a fabulous beast. In order to achieve a really magnificent coach I wanted to have a competition for the best state coach and to begin with a 'back wheels' competition as the first stage (see below). Out of this arose the story of a prince and princess betrothed to one another by their parents. The marriage feast was to be given in the newly built palace of the bridal couple and all the kings and queens in the world were invited. The father of the bride had planned a great wedding procession in which all the wedding guests in their state coaches would take part. The bride was to decide which equipage was the most beautiful and to decorate the royal victor with a garland.

Method

Preparation of the wax ground: with the exception of a marked-off margin, the whole sheet of the block is to be given an even coat of bright wax colours. The colours are applied in dense

Plate IV

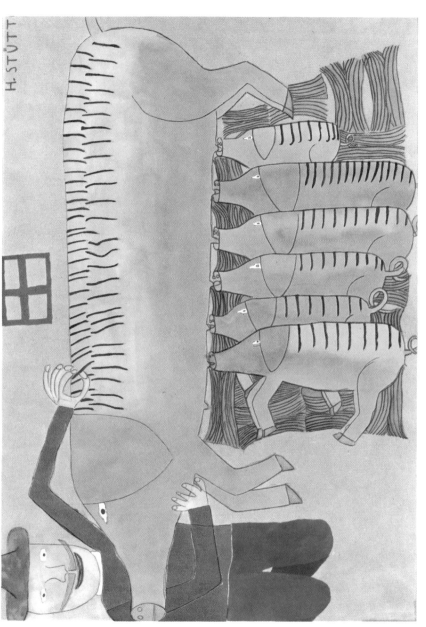

The Sow with Golden Bristles (E6), in poster colours, by an 11-year-old boy. Width 24 inches

Plate 13

a Fairy Coach (E5), wax engraving, by a 9-year-old boy. Width 24 inches

b Dance of Death (E9), lino cut, by a 19-year-old girl. Height 21 inches

Plate 14

a   Smugglers' Ship (E12), in poster colours, by a 15-year-old boy. Width 24 inches

*b   Natives Dancing (E13), resist painting, by a 13-year-old girl.
Width 23 inches*

hatching so that the background is invisible. Colours may either be varied at random or in conformity with a definite plan for the final engraving. The dark layer to be scratched away is applied over the light layer. To make the work easier, a layer of waterproof ink or dark designer's colour may be substituted for the upper wax layer. The engraving process: the under layer of wax can be revealed by means of an engraving tool such as a penknife, nail-file, etc. The engraving may consist of lines and areas.

Our fairy tale coach is drawn by a centaur or some other fabulous beast (Plate 13a). We begin with the 'back wheels' competition mentioned above. First the approximate arrangement of the whole picture must be known so that we can tell the position and size of the wheels. In order to proceed with due caution, we at first engrave only the outer circle to show the position and size of the back wheel. Then we can concentrate on the careful and richly inventive work of the first stage. This division of the task into stages is founded on the experience that a preliminary stage successfully completed determines the quality of succeeding stages. The fairy tale king who is to sit under such a magnificent canopy must be no less magnificent than his surroundings. The centaur that is harnessed to the coach of so noble a monarch must be just as nobly conceived.

The Sow with Golden Bristles (all ages)   E 6

> Painting in poster colours, from 10 upwards, with restricted palette. Drawing block, pencil, box of poster colours, brush.

This 'slow-witted peasant' story is not to be found in story books, as it was especially invented. A good pretext was needed for working with a palette restricted to tones of pink, ochre and gold. The climax of the story, the theme of our picture, is a scene in the pig-stye. The fat old sow lies with her rosy piglets on a bed of straw. The farmer was talked into buying her because she had 'gold in her bristles', a piece of sales talk which was not necessarily to be taken literally. With the growth of her family, the wealth of the farm appears to be increasing. But one night, yielding to his overwhelming curiosity, the farmer pulls out one of her bristles in order to estimate his wealth. The sequel, in which the farmer takes the seller to

103

court, of course also ends in disappointment for him, including the payment of legal costs.

Method

The introduction of a theme by a story or description is based on the conviction that healthy creative activity ought frequently to be illustrative. Still life or landscape painting is dominated throughout by its 'still' external theme; not so the painting of an event which develops to its climax and then passes away. In the depiction of an experience or event, it is essential to discover the pictorial moment which would be worthwhile to illustrate. To a painter or sculptor 'worthwhile' means in the highest degree capable of expression in visual terms.

In our story, the pig-stye scene is worthwhile in this sense. But before these pictorial qualities can be fully exploited, a mental process of translating the illustrative content into pictorial terms is required, a mental picture making. By means of this 'picture thinking' we discover that our picture will be better if the picture area is largely taken up by the central figure of the sow and if her litter, fairly tightly fitted into the remaining space, completes the picture (Colour Plate III). The figure of the farmer must also be included, but his hand and arm would suffice. Such considerations can best be conveyed in the course of an exchange of ideas with the class, in which the formal conditions governing the intended work are clearly brought out. This we call 'form discussion'.

Further themes: Snow White and the Seven Dwarfs; The Three Dogs (Hans Andersen, *The Tinderbox*); Aladdin and his Magic Lamp (1001 Nights); The Magic Ring (Leander); The Wild Swans (Andersen).

ALLEGORY AND PARABLE

E7 **The Knight, Death and the Devil (13 upwards)**

> Pen and ink drawing. Penholder and drawing nib or black ball-point pen, drawing block.

In order to learn to appreciate Dürer's masterly engraving from within, pupils are given the opportunity to draw the same theme. By 'from within' I mean: by being themselves faced with the same problem of graphic formulation and devoting all

104

their efforts to solving it in their own way. I am aware that the protagonists of a theory of art education infected by the illusion of modernism may condemn such teaching as backward-looking and old-fashioned. Those who recognise the deeper developmental needs of the young artist are not likely to waste much time on such transitory pseudo-theories of art education.

Method

A thorough examination of Dürer's engraving is not to be allowed until the task has been completed. A too exact previous knowledge of his formulation would lead only to inhibiting dependence. Each one must experience the spiritual content of the theme inwardly and personally before he can make any artistic statement of it. There exists no one who cannot respond to the symbolism of this theme; out of this response alone can a genuine picture arise.

Besides this spiritual response to the subject content, a second motivating condition is needful for artistic creation, namely the positive response of the pupil to his medium. Out of play with the pen and the exploration of its possibilities, out of the discovery of a 'pen palette', and the continual invention of new textures, out of the tensing and loosening of pictorial rhythms, the focussing and balancing of the picture masses evolves the characteristic unique life of a graphic composition, fusing into a living expression of experienced meaning, creating a new unity.

Scenes from 'The Little Prince' (14 upwards)   E 8

> Painting in poster colours with restricted palette and bristle brush. Drawing block, pencil or charcoal, box of poster colours, tube of white, bristle brush.

Antoine de Saint-Exupery's famous story book, *The Little Prince* contains a whole series of delightful picture-motifs: the little Prince and the Flower; the Prince and the King; the Prince and the Drunkard; the Prince and the Snake; the Prince on the Mountain; the Prince in the Rosegarden; the Prince and the Fox, etc. Of course these themes are suitable only for older children because of the ideas which are symbolically expressed in them (Colour Plate V). Moreover, like parables, they require a demonstrative style of treatment with numerous symbolic details, the significance of which could not be perceived by younger children.

Method

We intend to produce a series of pictures from which each pupil may choose his own particular subject. The connecting link between all the pictures, apart from the subject itself, will be the restriction of the colour to tones of red and blue and their admixture with black and white. We shall also all use a thick stippled style of painting with the bristle brush almost dry. We start with a large-scale charcoal drawing, all using the paper vertically (this is obligatory). The few figures in each picture are to fill the picture area as far as possible and there is to be no landscape or realistic background. What background remains is to be painted in one colour in freely rhythmic abstract forms.

We may divide the work into two main processes. The quality of the result depends first upon a good drawing and composition of the figures and secondly upon painting which, instead of blurring the effect of the drawing by its random use of colour, articulates it further by bold richly contrasting relationships of light and shade and fine harmonies.

E 9 **Dance of Death (15 upwards)**

> Series of lino cuts (see *150 Techniques in Art*, p. 57). Piece of lino, cutting tool, pane of glass, rubber roller, printing ink, absorbent paper, newspaper.

In the year 1538, Hans Holbein published his 'Pictures of Death' developing the current symbolic theme of the Dance of Death, in which the thought of generations had already found artistic expression, to a final classic formulation never equalled before or since. His pictures have lost none of their actuality, though the style of expression is now strange to us. The truism that 'in the midst of life we are in death' is just as present to us as it was to Holbein's contemporaries. Even the young, if they pause to consider, are conscious of this fact and can cite many instances of it. The expression of what lies in the depths of our consciousness has always been a function of art and will be for years.

Method

In a general discussion, we bring to mind the many occasions when modern man feels the nearness of death. Their number is impressive and disturbing. Death on the city road, on a main road in the country, on the sea, in the air, down the mine, on the skyscraper, in the family, at work, snatching the old and the young, the rich and the poor, the mighty and the humble, death who walks beside me. In this way each one discovers the theme he is going to attempt (Plate 13 b).

In our first sketches, we try to give it a form which is individual and at the same time universally valid. A desire to know the human skeleton by visual experience is spontaneously awakened. We come to the conclusion however that a simplified version fulfils the demands of the present picture and is also better adapted to our lino-cut technique. Large figures filling the picture area are advisable. When the best design has been drawn in pencil on the lino, the cutting is begun. We must be quite clear in our minds as to which parts of the picture are to be dark and which light in the final print.

Further themes: A Snake Fighting an Eagle; The Fox and the Crow (Aesop); 'Losing one's Head'; 'Leading someone up the Garden-Path'; 'Too many Cooks Spoil the Broth'; 'Putting the Cart before the Horse'; 'The Blind Leading the Blind'.

ADVENTURE AND BALLAD

Gang of Thieves (8 upwards) E 10

> Painting in poster or powder colours, group work. Drawing block 22 × 18 inches or loose sheets, box of poster colours, sable brush or powder mixed with a base, bristle brush, scissors, large sheet of wrapping paper, wallpaper paste, large flat brush, pins.

In a game of charades, children love pretending to be a gang of thieves, so here they will consider painting this subject a 'treat'. Is it because these characters, who at once emerge from our paintboxes, with their unshaven chins and caps pulled over their eyes, their gleaming knives and moneybags, their eyes fixed warily upon us as they slink stealthily past, have a likeable cockiness about them or that they make our flesh creep pleasurably?

Method

The various parts of the group work are painted separately. Each child is given a large sheet of paper on which he draws, in charcoal or pencil, the figure of a robber creeping from right to left. The figure is to fill the paper (used vertically) from top to bottom. In the final painting, we are careful to give sufficient colour contrast from light to dark, so that the figures will still be distinct from some distance. Once painted, the figures are cut out and arranged together on the background paper to form one large composition, a gang of thieves in Indian file. They may be arranged at regular intervals or in occasional closer groupings, may overlap or remain separated, so long as a lively effect is achieved. After various arrangements have been tried, we mark the final position of each figure with a sign or number. The back of each figure is then coated with paste, placed in position and pressed down with clean newspaper. The background can either be painted with a carefully chosen powder colour or enlivened with suitable objects (trees, a wood).

E 11 **Fight with an Octopus ('The Diver', after Schiller) (12 upwards)**

> Plaster intaglio or painting in poster colours (see *150 Techniques in Art*, p. 71). Boards for frame, pane of glass, large bowl, wire broom, plaster of Paris, pencil, penknife.

Schiller's ballad 'The Diver' is to supply our theme which is full of movement and complete in itself and therefore suitable for a plaster relief. The sharply defined motif demands a clear silhouette-like presentation of the moving bodies of the diver and of the octopus, its tentacles spread out star-wise, that is, in full view. Only in this way can each figure be distinct, pictured in the flat as a 'prototype' and therefore suitable for a relief. The meeting of the figures in combat must not involve too much overlapping: they must rather be shown side by side, linked by a few grappling movements.

Method

The drawing of the design and the filling of the large frame (about 20 inches square and one inch deep) with plaster (mix equal parts of plaster and water in the bowl with a wire broom and pour on to glass surrounded by wooden frame) are our first tasks. When the plaster plaque has been taken out (20 minutes) the smooth underside is used as the right side on which the design is drawn to suitable scale in pencil. The lines of the drawing are then scored with the point of a knife held diagonally to the plaster. The contours of the bodies are then dug out deeper, in rounded concave form towards the centres, and sharply, almost perpendicularly, inclining outwards very slightly at the body contour lines against the 'background' which is the remaining raised part of the plaque. This is how this ancient (Egyptian) pictorial form, the low relief with a raised background, is produced. This technique may also be used to produce a raised, or ordinary, relief picture if, from the point when the first lines have been cut, they are deepened outwards. In cases of unavoidable overlapping of forms (e.g. of the diver with the fish) the 'nearest' of the two forms is continued normally, the further form cut a little deeper than normal. One should not be concerned with realistic accuracy or representation. Clear-cut body contours and carefully graded rounding of the figures fulfil the essential demands of clarity, even if a few mistakes in intersection should occur.

Smugglers' Ship attacking a coastguard Station (13 upwards)   E 12

> Painting in poster colours. Drawing block, pencil, box of poster colours, brush.

A theme for boys only: a little harbour jetty with a customs station on it. The smugglers' vessel has put in unnoticed in the half-light before dawn, but is seen at the last moment by the coast-guards; a man-to-man fight ensues. Will the smugglers be defeated? Some are falling into the sea, others have been overpowered; but the fight still goes on.

The essential features of the picture (jetty, little house, ship) must be well related to one another in the picture area (whether it be used vertically or horizontally). This formal aspect of the composition must be considered first. It is to reveal the central dramatic action, the fight. Thus the formal and the dramatic demands of the picture control our attention at the same time.

Method

We are still at the preliminary drawing stage. All our powers of representation are called into play; no detail is unimportant: the pier as a firmly knit structure of wood and stone with bollards for mooring the ships, steps leading down to the water: the coastguard station, its structure also defined in detail, its doors and windows flung open, men pushing their way in and out: the ship with its sharp contours and sturdy masts, its sails furled, the complex rigging with ladders and ropes and, high above, the dreaded pirate flag, the terror of the seas (Plate 14 a).

The second stage of the work, the colouring, demands no less essential, but more 'leisuredly' effort. It differs from the first stage in that the most exacting decisions have been made and that now the completion of some parts of the work requires manual skill rather than mental concentration. In contrast with the first stage, singing or listening to a story are premissible accompaniments to the work, which makes fingers nimbler.

Further themes: The Lion-tamer; Circus Acrobats; Pyramid of Circus Riders; Pursued by a Herd of Elephants; Robin Hood and the Sheriff; Climbing the North Face of Mont Blanc; Divers Hunting for Treasure.

EXOTIC ADVENTURE

E 13 **Natives Dancing (all ages)**

> Resist painting (see *150 Techniques in Art*, p. 84). Drawing block, box of poster colours, brush, waterproof ink or designer's colour (dark), large flat brush or fixative spray.

The simple discovery that waterproof ink will not take on top of a painting in poster colours but is fast on plain paper produced this delightful technique. Figures and objects in the picture are painted in poster colours while the background (and parts of the figures which are intended to come out black) is left plain. The whole is then quickly painted or sprayed with waterproof black ink (with a fixative spray). When it is dry, the ink will have flaked away from the coloured parts of the picture. With a hard brush, or even more easily under the tap by smoothing with a wet hand, the ink can be completely removed, leaving the colours clear.

Method

Our natives are brown (black figures would become grey in the course of the washing off process but could also look quite effective on a black ground). Straw skirts and headdresses, bangles and other bodily adornments, such as tattooing, etc., cannot be added as a second coat to the painting as they would be removed in the washing off process. All the painting must be done in one layer; that is, any decoration must be applied directly to the paper if it is to survive the washing. In contrast therefore with our usual poster painting technique, we begin the decoration as soon as a simple pencil drawing has shown the positions of the figures. The figures of the group of dancers, who are the focus of the picture, are large and fill the composition (Plate 14b). Straw huts, palm trees or animals can fill any incomplete parts of the picture, but should be drawn without intersections.

Red Indian's Island (10-14)   E 14

Painting in poster colours. Drawing block, pencil, box of poster colours, brush.

The 10-14 age-group still choose to live their fantasy life in the distant, exotic world of imaginary Red Indians. The freedom and natural adventurous life which they believe to exist among these tribes is imitated for some time in many of the games of girls and boys alike until eventually the reading of adventure stories becomes a substitute. Our picture is to give an exotic and colourful living centre to this dream world of play.

This is possible only through a creative effort which demands not only all our willing enthusiasm, but also an unusual amount of time and energy, and thereby becomes an important and unforgettable experience. We intend to devote about two months, in which we have two hours weekly, to this task.

It is therefore essential to divide the task into stages upon which we can concentrate one by one and, at the same time, to circumscribe it clearly, so that it does not grow out of hand. These considerations decide our method.

Method
The Indians have landed their canoes on a small island where they have already set up wigwams in the shelter of a few tropical trees. They are to be engaged in all sorts of activities: fishing, shooting birds, and mooring their boats and tents. The coast of the island, like a 'frame within the picture', with its many little bays, helps to prevent the picture from becoming amorphous. The drawing stage begins with the careful mapping

111

of its coast. The addition of small carefully differentiated trees is another separate task. Various kinds of trees are depicted one after another, each kind being studied and planned according to its various features (angle of the branches, mode of growth and density of foliage, shapes and division of the leaves, large or small, etc.). Next the positions of the wigwams are carefully selected. Intersections between tents and trees are made, which produce a more lively grouping and a clearer spatial relationship between the objects in the picture. The boats are already moored, and now the camp life can begin.

We begin the stages of the painting with the objects. The island itself and the water are best painted in terms of surface structure (reeds on the shore, tufts of grass on the land, waves in the water) so that too massive a background colour may not outweigh or destroy the intended effect of the objects and figures themselves.

E 15 **The Great Chief (10 upwards)**

> Painting in poster colour and subsequent translation into some other suitable medium such as fabric or leather appliqué, mosaic of natural materials, etc. (see *150 Techniques in Art,* pp. 44 ff., 52, 55).

Themes with one or a few large figures, have among many advantages, which make them appear particularly suitable for the middle and upper classes, that of being easily translatable into other techniques. By such a translation, a design or finished work can often be greatly enhanced in the decorative and textural sense. One should also bear in mind that some light sketch or worked out picture often contains detail which, quite by chance, would be wonderfully effective in some particular medium and be well worth translating. Teachers gain much by cultivating an eye for such treasures which surround them.

Method

It was this idea which prompted the present theme. Whether we set the class to make small sketches or large poster colour paintings of our theme, The Great Chief, there will always be, among the results, many which clearly call for translation into a decorative technique, limited by a more resistant medium. We can allow such a design to be redrawn in charcoal on wrapping paper to be made into a mural-size fabric appliqué. Alternatively, we can repeat the lines of the design with the point of a knife on a layer of size and sand spread on a large plywood base, as the foundation for a mosaic of natural materials, with patches of various coloured pebbles, crumbs of brick or coke, splinters of slate, etc. A firm of leather-goods' manufacturers may supply scraps of leather of various colours which could be used for leather appliqué pasted to strong cardboard with cold size.

Further themes: The Maharajah; The Oasis; A Procession of Sedan Chairs; A Flotilla of Outriggers; Jungle Princess; Sphinx and Pyramids; Masked Dancers.

F THEMES OF FANTASY AND UTOPIAN DREAM

FABULOUS BEINGS

F 1   **Merman (all ages)**

> Direct painting in poster colours. Drawing block, box of poster colours, brush.

A poor peasant has to cut wood in the forest on the shores of an enchanted lake. His old axe, his only axe, falls into the water. Bubbles rise to the surface and suddenly the terrifying head of the merman appears. His arm is outstretched; he holds up a silver axe: 'Is this thine?' 'No, that is not mine.' Next a golden axe is offered. 'No, that is not mine either.' The peasant finally accepts his own rusty axe but is given the golden axe. A rich peasant wants to get one too, goes to the lake and throws in his oldest axe. He refuses the silver axe and claims the golden one as his. On the way home he tests the blade against a tree. The axe flies out of his hand, cuts off his leg and disappears.

Method

Younger children may choose their own scene from the story to illustrate. Older ones can limit their subject and depict, for instance, a large figure of the Merman alone rising from the water. His streaming hair is interwoven with water weeds and decorated with a few waterhen's feathers. The head fills the whole picture. Direct painting in strongly contrasting imaginative colour produces a vividly expressive picture. The large glowing eyes, the savage teeth, the gruesome hair and matted beard, the nightmare adornment of the head all heighten the fantastic effect.

Themes of fantasy have a liberating influence on inhibited children. Where the unconventional and strange is right, they can no longer fear being wrong. All concern with fidelity to nature fades away. Moreover themes of magic and dream awaken a child's innate love of the extraordinary and his desire to create and feast his eyes upon something 'never seen on land or sea'. The excitement of creating something from fantasy need not prevent the work from being well planned. The new

114

freedom, on the contrary, liberates energies which, no longer held back by other demands, can all be used to create a picture of outstanding quality.

Martians (10 upwards)

> Pendrawing. Drawing block, drawing pen or ballpoint, fountain pen, etc.

Indelible drawing is occasionally useful. If such drawing with a pen or brush is combined with a theme of fantasy, two means of art education are simultaneously active, liberating the child from his inhibitions in drawing and also helping the tentative draughtsman to bold decisive line. For it helps one to overcome an exaggerated fear of deciding on a line, if the decision is known to be irrevocable; one learns to forget the possibility of constant correction. Besides it is almost impossible to draw something 'wrong' when the drawing is an expression of fantasy, not to be measured against some real norm, but intended to be 'unreal'.

Method

We know nothing about whatever life there may be on Mars. What may exist there of organic life, which may even be endowed with reason, leading its own life, is still far beyond the exploration even of our astronautic age. In fantasy however, we can easily travel through space and invent for ourselves the most extraordinary 'contemporaries' to people it. Not only the Utopian imaginations of writers but also the untrammelled spirit of schoolchildren can imagine beings of daringly complex capacities who live an equally daring and complex life in a strange environment. Our theme is to inspire the class to thrilling encounters with beings of their own invention.

Masks and Grotesque Faces (10 upwards)

> Paper relief in masking technique on clay or other modelling material (see *150 Techniques in Art,* p. 74). Dug or bought clay, or modelling material; newspaper, wallpaper paste, 2 large bowls, powder or poster colours.

A lump of clay or malleable material in the hand of a human being has the power to set that hand in movement, the movement of shaping and moulding. The power that lies in the media of graphic and plastic art cannot be experienced more directly than this. To this perfect medium we add the perfect theme: masks, a theme which has its own wonderfully liberating effect. It allows any exaggeration and caricature that fantasy may dictate; nothing can really be wrong. Perhaps hitherto unused talents will be manifest, for the manipulation of plastic material is an inborn need in man just as creative fantasy is.

Method

In plastic relief modelling, the forms can be either built up or shaped out. We shape the main features with bold emphasis: the nose broad or pointed, long or short, hooked or rounded; the lips thick or narrow, the mouth wide or pouting, the eyes protruding or sunken, the forehead shelving or bulging, the chin jutting or receding. All these different possibilities in the formation of the mask can be considered in an opening discussion. We may drop the hint that a mask face, unlike a flat drawing of a face, must be strongly convex at the centre, so that the forehead forms a half-circle and the cheeks recede on either side so that a sculptural effect is achieved.

The finished clay relief is carefully masked with about 10 layers of newspaper the size of the palm of the hand. The first layer is dipped in water, the succeeding layers in paste. When completely dried, the mask can be lifted from the clay. The resulting papier-mâché relief can be painted.

Further themes: A Bird-Man; The Devil and his Grandmother; Puppet Theatre; Conjuring up Ghosts; Robot Family in a Robot Forest; The Sorcerer; Witches Falling from their Brooms; Wild Men; Carnival Figures; The Canterville Ghost from Oscar Wilde's story.

FABULOUS BEASTS

F 4   **Fantastic Birds (all ages)**

Direct painting in poster or ordinary powder colours. Drawing block (or 'scrap' paper), box of poster colours and sable brush (or powder colours and bristle brush).

A theme must be 'dressed up' as a story if it is to be adapted to the junior school, unless, like 'My Mother' it is firmly based on immediate experience. With the middle and upper classes it is a different matter. Here the children are capable of artistic reaction at the mere spark of an idea from the teacher, without recourse to fairy tales or immediate visual experience. Recognition of these differences and conditioning factors is the true basis of sympathetic understanding in the teaching of art to children. Our theme 'Fantastic Birds' is among the 'trump' subjects. This need not prevent us from building a truly child-like framework for it. Very diverse introductions are possible, so long as they create a teacher-pupil relationship and an atmosphere of united effort.

Method

We start with a brush drawing using only one strong colour (black, red, blue, green, but not yellow or white). We emphasise the fantastic element by the free combination and exaggeration of details *(Cover design)*. The bird's beak, for instance, can be long and hooked or else short and straight; it may even have more than one beak, since it may have more than one head. Nothing is impossible in a fantastic bird. Great diversity is possible: the head can be gigantic or very tiny, the neck thin or thick or may disappear into the body completely. The body itself is highly variable, as also the construction, length and thickness of the legs, which can be feathered, hairy or scaly. There is no reason why a fantastic bird should not have a fish tail or even two, or a bushy tail like a colt. A lion's mane may adorn its neck, and, instead of a beak, it may have the fearful jaws of a dragon. All is unconfined mutability in contrast with familiar fixed reality. All the same, in order not to depart from the bird theme entirely, the splendour of its plumage will remain dominant. All the characteristics and details can be expressed in the drawing. Every line drawn should make a clear statement, however fantastic. Confused lines and scribbles are out of place even here. The elaborate drawing will be painted and further enhanced by the careful organisation of rich colours.

Dance of the Hell-Hounds (12 upwards)   F 5

Wax engraving (see *150 Techniques in Art*, p. 37). Wax crayons, drawing block, penknife, or nail-file, possibly waterproof ink and bristle brush.

Dogs and children are often good friends, but everyone imagines hell-hounds as terrifying, bristly creatures with wolfish eyes, snarling fangs and tearing teeth and claws. If we could watch them dancing from a suitable distance, it might be frightening and fascinating at the same time. Of course it is hellishly dark all around them, but one can see them glowing from within.

Method

The technique of wax engraving is ideal for showing our hell-hounds glowing out of the darkness. First we must prepare the ground. In close hatching we put on the layer of wax for engraving, leaving no paper visible. We let the colours vary at random but use only light colours (including blue; although it sometimes seems rather dark, in some makes of crayon it gets lighter). We avoid brown and black, as the second layer of wax, the layer to be scratched away, which completely covers the first layer, must be either brown or black. A layer of waterproof ink or powder colour (with size) may be substituted for the second layer of wax to speed the process. Colour which forms little drops on the surface of the wax can be brought into contact with it by strong rubbing with a bristle brush.

A very light outline drawing in pencil is enough to help in the arrangement of the figures on the dark ground. The engraving process is scraping away the uppermost layer of wax to reveal the coloured layer on the paper. For our present theme, a simple line engraving is best. We therefore avoid scratching away any areas of colour and fill up the inner areas of the figures with bristly hairs. For the colour of the bodies the 'colour' or surface-structure is substituted. Only the eyes, the noses with dark nostrils, the teeth or lolling tongues are scratched out in complete colour and so given emphasis. The background is left dark.

F 6   **The Fish Prince (all ages)**

> Painting in poster colours. Drawing block, box of poster colours, brush.

The fish has been one of the most successful themes of art teaching ever since teachers have cared about free creative art. Like the other simple theme of cocks, it holds such a wealth of pictorial possibilities that no art-course worthy of the name can

118

Plate 15

a The Fish Prince (F6), glass mosaic, by a student teacher. Width 28 inches

b The Torch-bearer (F8), in poster colours, by an 11-year-old boy. Height 22 inches

c Fantastic Ships (F12), in poster colours, by a 13-year-old boy. Width 24 inches

Plate 16

a *Volcanic Eruption (F13), in powder colours, by a 14-year-old boy. Width 21 inches*

b *Geranium (G4), in poster colours, by an 11-year-old boy. Height 24 inches*

c *Wooden Wheelbarrow (G3), pen drawing, by a 15-year-old boy. Width 14 inches*

Plate V

The Little Prince (E8), in poster colours, by a 16-year-old girl. Height 26 inches

do without it. An active and original teacher is always finding new enlivening variants, which, while using proven methods, counteract any tendency to fall into a rut.

Method

What prince meets with no adventures? What king's son does not fall into the sorcerer's clutches through his foolhardiness? What sorcerer could not transform a prince into a fish by a spell from which only the love of a pure maiden can free him? For the present however, he must remain under the spell though he may wear his crown. He has retained his human face, and his arms and legs are to be seen dangling between his fins (Plate 15 a). If we look closely, perhaps we may recognise the princely cloak that he once wore. His royal lineage is still apparent through his disguise; such melancholy splendour can belong to no ordinary fish. The figure of the fish-prince is to fill the whole picture area (used horizontally) and is to have its 'natural' proportions. A preliminary pencil draw-in will determine the proportions and details but need not delay the painting long. A thick coat of poster paint gives the basic colours. Details such as the scales on the body, the fine structure of the fins and tail and the facial features can be added in opaque colour with an almost dry brush.

Further themes: A Duel of Dragons; In the Land of the Birdmen; Fantastic Deep-Sea Fish; The Loch Ness Monster; The Martian Horse; The Firebird over the City; Carnival Procession of Animal Masks; The Robot Dog; Prehistoric Animals; The Bird of Death.

WONDROUS AND FANTASTIC OBJECTS

Fantastic Flowers (8 upwards)   F 7

> Painting in poster colours. Drawing block, pencil, box of poster colours, brush.

A whole bouquet of fantastic flowers in a vase—what an exciting creative theme! Where do they come from? Perhaps from a fairy tale invented by the children or the teacher. Perhaps they simply came to life of themselves, one by one, without any other purpose than to embody fresh exotic beauty.

Each one glows with the joy of having been invented by us. For each of us can be like God and create new flowers that did not exist before. Man was given the joy of creating; this joy will fill our classroom.

Method

During the first week of her marriage, a young queen each day gave her husband a different flower which had never been seen before. Each one had a particular virtue which gave delight to the young king while he was occupied with matters of state. They gave him perfume and nectar, rang like silvery bells at his approach, bowed when he entered the room, or drove away tiresome councillors, who began to sneeze if they approached a certain flower. But when the king approached the last flower of all to inhale its perfume, he fell into a deep sleep in which he relived the first week of his marriage with its miraculous flowers.

One can elaborate this fairy tale and tell it in detail as pretext for a division of the work into successive tasks, stopping at the description of each flower to be painted. This method is particularly suitable for classes who have not formed the habit of concentration.

F 8   **The Torch-bearer (10 upwards)**

> Painting in poster colours. Drawing block, pencil, box of poster colours, brush.

Many towns in the Rhineland have, once a year, a children's torch procession, which is preceded by a lamp competition in which many enthusiastic young artists take part. The children devise lamps in the form of fantastic human masks, heads of fabulous beasts, of all sorts of real animals, and even in the form of architecture. A close-up photograph of the beaming prizewinner appears in due course in the local newspaper; only his face is visible and his hands holding his prize-winning lamp. The printed label with 'First Prize' is prominently displayed.

Method

We are going to have our kind of lamp competition: 'The Front Page Photograph' is our title and each pupil is to paint a self-portrait, his own head and his hands holding the handle of the wonderful glowing lamp that swings above his head (Plate 15 b). The prize label bears no inscription for we cannot tell who will be the winner until all the 'photographs' are finished.

As no particular kind of lamp is specified, each child is left entirely free to follow his own fantasy. The idea that only the creator of something impressive and amazing can hope to win the prize, spurs their imaginations. The treasures of fantasy and invention that lie hidden among a class of 30-40 children will be revealed. Only the teacher knows in advance that he will have to distribute a whole row of prizes.

Space Station (12 upwards) F 9

> White resist painting on black (see *150 Techniques in Art,* p. 83). Drawing block, pencil, tube of white paint, sable brush, waterproof ink, large flat brush or fixative spray.

It is worth noting that the widespread technical interest of modern youth, far from being limited to real objects, expresses itself as readily in Utopian fantasies. Today the immediate field upon which their constructive dreams are concentrated is the conquest of space, which has inspired many stories and novels of the past, and, the nearer the possibility of achievement appears to be, the more glowingly it is coloured by the dawn of realisation. Designs are even now coming into being on the drawing boards of the greatest engineers in the world, which are to lead to the construction of the first space stations.

Method

The technical has no place in the realm of art unless, through transformation, it becomes an artistic creation. Its function is then no longer technical but artistic. Thus we are not concerned with planning a realisable space station—how could we?—but with presenting an artistic vision of an object of the technical world. Our version of the 'technical' is only an artistic symbol for the real technical. Its pictorial function is to be a rhythmic visual experience.

In the preliminary faint pencil drawing, rulers and compasses may be used. Next the lines are painted with a solution of white paint. Flat areas of the structure also receive a watery white solution. Now we cover the whole white painting on the white paper with waterproof ink, either with a large flat brush (painting quickly so that it has no time to dissolve the white paint) or with the fixative spray. (The spraying technique should be visible; a medium tone may be used.) When the ink is dry, the white lines can be washed clean (under running water), while the watery white areas have a misty veiled appearance.

Further themes: The Crown of a Fairy-Tale King; Treasures at the Bottom of the Sea; The Twittering Machine *(cf.* Paul Klee); The Bewitched Car; The Universal Musical Instrument; The Magic Pack of Cards; A Dream Doll; Festival of Wonderful Lamps; Scarecrow.

THE WORLD OF MYSTERY AND ENCHANTMENT

F 10 **Mosque of the 30 Minarets (10 upwards)**

> Painting in poster colours, communal work. 'Scrap' paper or sketching block, box of poster colours, brush, scissors, wallpaper paste, large sheet of wrapping paper 40×60 inches, powder colours.

The 30 best architects in the world build the 30 minarets of the most beautiful mosque in the world, in which the Sultan prays to Allah for the happiness which he has never known. While he is praying, a monk appears to him and tells him to search for Gisor, the nightingale. As he is too old, he sends his three sons to seek the bird. The eldest son is persuaded to buy a false nightingale. The second son gets another nightingale by dishonest means. The youngest son wanders about for three years, lured on by a maiden who sings to him in his dreams: 'Go on with your journey and you will find what you seek.' After facing many perils, he finds the maiden and the nightingale in a garden enclosed by a golden cage, the door of which closes behind him. The nightingale now flies to his father, but the old man has just died, for 'Everyone must seek the nightingale for himself'.

Method

One of the pictorial highlights of the story is the dedication of the mosque with the procession of the 30 architects, at whose head walks the Sultan, the most magnificent figure of all. Each pupil takes a sheet of paper of agreed size, and draws a minaret, either tall and slim or short and sturdy, with windows, balconies, decorations and a beautiful dome. When the minarets have been drawn, painted and cut out, the architects are drawn on smaller pieces of paper. Meanwhile a large background sheet of wrapping paper has been covered with a coat of deep

126

blue powder colour. The minarets and figures are tried out in various positions, grouped and overlapping (the lower towers with doors in front, the tallest at the back), until a well-composed architectural whole in the upper part of the picture and well-ordered procession in the lower half have been achieved. We mark the positions of the various parts and paste them down.

Girl in an Enchanted Garden (15 upwards) F 11

> Painting in thick poster colour on a coloured ground. Drawing block, pencil, box of poster colours, sable brush.

As in a dream, the girl wanders among the strange vegetation of an enchanted garden. What hidden mysteries will it reveal; what may be hidden behind the next bush she passes? She holds out her hand as if to ward off her fear, and looks about her as if for protection. But the whispering life of the plants and the soundless movements of the creatures are not hostile, merely invisible and mysterious. Is that something sleeping on the ground? Is that something standing in the shadow? What is it that seems to glow and to look out at her? Can she not sense the waiting of a host of living things? Are they not gathering, whispering? The night is at hand.

Method

We begin by mixing enough medium-toned colour, to cover the whole twilight background of our picture. We mix black and a little white poster paint with either a greenish or a reddish colour producing an even colour which we apply slowly over the slightly tilted surface of the block, from top to bottom. When the ground is dry, we sketch lightly in pencil the positions of the main masses and the individual objects in our composition. The painting will define outlines and elaborate forms to produce a complete, closely-knit picture.

The vagueness of our introduction and our omission of any definite detail was intentional, so that personal fantasy and invention could develop unhindered. No definite story, no event points in any preordained direction. Thus, the individual can dream his own dream in the spacious realm of the unknown.

The medium tone is a good ground on which to paint light and shade allowing a wide range of contrast.

127

Fantastic Ships (10 upwards)

> Painting in poster colours. Drawing block, pencil, box of poster colours, brush.

As a rule a class develops as much fantasy as their teacher possesses, since he stimulates theirs. The attitude 'My pupils aren't up to that standard' usually implies 'I'm not up to the standard of my class', but this fact is not always recognised. The question is: 'how am I to stimulate my imagination as a painter and as a teacher?' The answer is firstly by losing myself in the spirit of the theme, and secondly, by losing myself in the minds of my pupils.

1. The theme: a ship is recognisable as such by its hull and its superstructure. In the course of history, countless variants have been developed without these characteristics ever being lost. How much more numerous must the variants be when there is no longer any question of real or realisable ships but only of the free inventions of our fantasy Plate 15 c)?

2. The pupils: In my pupils I sense a slumbering energy which longs to be awakened; I know that their spirits have hidden wings that long to spread and to use that awakened energy to rise above everything which is not of their own essence and to explore realms of freedom.

Method

That is why I give my pupils no fixed criteria, no preconceived ideas, when it is a question of using their wings. On the contrary, I encourage them to fly off on their own wings to their own rich world of pictures, and to use their own powers to give form to the wealth of images they discover there. The task of education therefore is the task of awakening and of sending off on the way. The task of artistic creation is the task of rising up by oneself, seeing for oneself, finding oneself and realising oneself. Each pupil has the task of creating one variation on the theme of fantastic ships out of the infinite wealth of possibility. His personal task is to define its form as completely and to make its colour as vivid as he can.

Further themes: The City Under the Sea (Atlantis); Comic Landscape; The Enchanted Castle; The Heavenly Jerusalem; Trees Walking; Moon-Garden; Masquerade of Icebergs; Dream Mountains; Fantastic Industrial Landscape; Rendez-vous of Heavenly Bodies.

Volcanic Eruption (12 upwards) F 13

> Painting in poster colours. Drawing block, box of poster colours, brush.

If we want to get our pupils to talk to us, we have only to ask them to recount their dreams. The dream world of children, like that of adults, is full of archetypal images in which the terrifying is side by side with the familiar. The pleasure a child has in relating even his most terrifying dreams arises from the unconscious wish to free himself by verbal objectification from those dark forces which threaten to overpower him in dreams, and thus to be better able to withstand them in future. Thus the telling and also the pictorial representation of such things is essential to mental health.

Method

Fortunately the cooling earth seldom allows us to enjoy the sight of a volcanic eruption nowadays. In our fantasy however we can easily picture to ourselves the earth bursting open, the seething eruption of fire and burning lava, the fountains of smoke and showers of ashes, and can paint the scene in all its vehemence and cruel beauty (Plate 16a). The expression both of the elemental natural event itself and of the ideas it evokes calls for direct painting in broad, strongly pigmented flowing colours. Rich contrasts from light and dark heighten the expressive effect. Only thick textured, well pigmented paint can adequately represent the primitive violence of matter in such a picture. Apart from some guidance on these lines, we would give free rein to each individual in the working out of his own idea and painting procedure.

Pursued by Night (12 upwards) F 14

> Painting in poster colours on a coloured ground. Drawing block, box of poster colours, brush.

Dreams and fantasies of pursuit are familiar to most people from their own experience. Some monster or terrifying figure is behind them. In darkness or twilight, through strange, uncanny landscapes, hindered by every sort of bizarre obstacle, the dreamer tries to escape from his dreaded pursuers, who are always just behind him.

Method

We would suggest a background of a medium tone, for the twilight or semi-darkness. Each pupil must first mix enough of the colour on his palette (lid of the paintbox). (It is easier to apply the colour with a large round bristle brush, and best and quickest of all with a large flat brush about 2 inches wide, of which a class would need only about four or five.)

We have now produced tinted paper, which, when dry—or alternatively at its damp stage—is an excellent background for a night scene of adventure. The medium tone sets off the sharp contrast of light and shade; we can paint the shapes of night straight on to it in darker tones, and, here and there introduce a ghostly light by means of areas, lines and structures in colours varied by the addition of more or less white from consistency to transparency.

F 15 **In the Temple of the Idols (12 upwards)**

> Direct painting in poster colours. Drawing block, box of poster colours, brush.

In the children's library is a section which attracts readers of about 12 because it satisfies the desire of those who have not quite reached adolescence for a graphic and colourful experience of alien worlds in the form of exciting adventure stories. Through these tales, European boys and girls can live another life of fantasy among distant peoples, the beauties and terrors of whose strange ways of life touch their romantic hearts and lure their receptive minds into the glowing or shadowy realms of bygone or exotic cults and civilisations. It is not surprising if our pupils have a far more vivid picture of exotic civilisations than we who, in our preoccupation with immediate needs and realities, have long ago forgotten what does not touch our own lives.

Method

Our lightening wings of fantasy carry us in a matter of seconds from the classroom to the mysterious temple of the idols, which no ordinary mortal may enter and live. Some of the priests of the temple are prostrated before the gigantic statues of their gods, their heads touching the floor. The immortals

130

look down upon their worshippers with veiled and threatening gaze, expressing their silent life by enigmatic or terrifying gestures. Behind the images, the walls of the temple are sunk in depths of mysterious shadow, whence we catch the gleam of one or two of the innumerable carvings and arabesques with which the interior is encrusted.

Before starting on a theme of this kind, it is sometimes useful to give oneself up entirely to its visualisation by a deliberate exercise of one's fantasy, that is, by laying one's head on the desk, buried in one's arms, and letting oneself fall into a trance in which one can see the images clearly. In artistic creation, what is true of imaginative representation of objects in general is also true of the representation of fantastic objects, namely, that we can and should first acquire a clear idea of the objects by 'looking', in order to have this visual image ready in our minds for translation into a picture. The only difference is that with fantastic subjects we look inwards instead of at external objects.

Further themes: The Nightmare; Haunted Wood; Lunar Landscape; The Wolf's Gorge; The Garden of Carnivorous Plants; Lost in the Labyrinth; The War of the Elements; City of the Dead; A Gathering of Grisly Characters; A Stormy Night.

STILL LIFE

G 1   **Miscellaneous Tools (10 upwards)**

> Painting in poster colours. Drawing block, pencil, box of poster colours, brush.

The workaday world in which children grow up is and has always been a world of tools, which takes the indispensable hammer, pliers, scissors and knife for granted. At first they are handed or lent to the child by an adult, but soon penknife, saw, drill and hammer become important personal belongings to many a schoolboy. School or private tool-boxes will supply illustrative material to be studied for our art exercise.

Method

The success of a drawing of an object studied beforehand is based not upon continued observation of the object but upon an acquired visual image of it. The object is therefore put out of sight while it is being drawn. (Drawing in front of the subject is possible only for those who have acquired the capacity to free the impression of inessentials. The average pupil, if required to draw an object from life, would only try to copy it by adding individual parts one by one, producing not a unified drawing but disconnected fragments.) Further study of the subject without drawing may be allowed occasionally in the course of the work should any difficulty arise which could be solved thereby. The more intensively the formation of the visual image is fostered by practical handling, technical observation and verbal description of a still-life subject, the more characterful the resulting artistic formulation.

With the objective artistic description of the subject must be combined the creative achievement of pictorial composition. The task is to relate the objects in the picture through the directions of their lines and the balance of their masses and colours. There must be no ugly gaps in the composition, no conflicting lines, no unbalanced masses, no warring of the colours. Balance and unity, harmony and reconciliation, however, can be achieved only by the diligent use and development of our sense of form, never by calculation, precept and theory.

Large Seashells (10 upwards) G 2

> Painting in poster colours, from 14 upwards also resist painting (see *150 Techniques in Art*, p. 83). Drawing block, pencil, tube of white poster colour, waterproof ink, sable brush, large flat brush or fixative spray.

In contrast with the foregoing strictly linear theme, the theme 'Seashells', is vivid and paintable in its forms and colours. Shell forms are usually highly complex with their modelling and three-dimensional solidity. It is this very fact which makes their naive translation by younger children into a two-dimensional pattern so delightful. Work should begin with a thorough study of the complex shapes and colours of the shells without reference to their visual peculiarities as objects in space. This advice, though it may seem a selfcontradiction, involves an important principle of art teaching. With younger children we consider only those characteristics of an object, which are integral parts of its pictured being, and not its accidental appearance which is subject to the constant change of perspective foreshortening and distortion. This is completely in keeping with our ordinary naive way of seeing things as we 'know them to be'. In the case of shells it means that we observe their swelling and growing smaller again, twisting and curving, forming themselves into ringlets, grooves, knobs and pointed horns, having certain colours, both light and dark, but not the complex intersection of their lines within themselves and with one another, overlappings, foreshortenings, reflections of light and complex shadow effects. This way of looking, which we now avoid, belongs to a later, impressionistic approach to art.

Method

There is one 'good view' of every object (possibly more) according to the artistic stage (e.g. horse—from the side; salamander—from above). Younger pupils find the 'good view' of shells without hesitation. A pencil or charcoal drawing, showing the size and disposition of the objects, may be corrected a little until a balanced composition is achieved. The inner lines of a shell are best drawn with its outline. A broad painting of the basic colours of the shells follows. Coloured markings and structure can be overpainted. The table top, possibly the wall-paper, or window, or simply one neutral colour serves as background. For the white resist technique, proceed as under F9.

G 3 **Wooden Wheelbarrow (14 upwards)**

> Pen drawing. Drawing block, pencil, penholder with drawing nib—or black ballpoint pen—drawing ink.

For drawing we choose subjects which attract by the diversity of their outline and surfaces. Though a wheelbarrow is a familiar object, we study it afresh. Picturesque weatherbeaten ones are hard to find, but a new toy wheelbarrow will do as well. Two aspects concern us: its outline, simple, yet with lines going in several directions, and the grain of its wood; to each side supporting legs are attached; the long wooden handles for lifting and pushing pass under it to the axle of the strong wheel, with its stout spokes and hub (Plate 16c).

Method

When the wheelbarrow has been sufficiently studied, its cubic structure is most usually and easily represented from memory as if viewed diagonally from above, to show that the body is hollow. This is a comparatively advanced task in drawing but can be tackled from the age of 14. The problems must be solved by each pupil in his own way, without criticism of shortcomings in the perspective. When the outlines of all its parts have been related to form the whole, we draw the graining of the wood carefully and sensitively. A well-composed group of several overlapping wheelbarrows makes an even more effective picture. A preliminary composition sketch in pencil for the grouping is advisable.

Further themes: Musical Instruments; Bunch of Keys; Writing Materials; Bottles and Vases; Typewriter and Accessories; Pair of Skis; Baskets and Boxes; Chairs and Stools; Painting Equipment; Carpenter's tools.

Geranium (10 upwards)

Painting in poster colours. Drawing block, pencil, box of poster colours, brush.

For the middle school the theme 'Geranium' is a good introduction to subjects from nature. We proceed from a detailed examination of the elements to consideration of the subject as a whole. The elements are easy to examine separately: the leaf and its stem, inflorescence and blossoms, main stalk and its branches, flowerpot and soil. Each is studied in its characteristic or complete aspect, undistorted by accidents of perspective. It is not the biological characteristics of the plant, but its form and colour that matter in the art lesson. These are to be noted thoroughly and described verbally. For example: the leaf has a general circular form with a definite number of main and of smaller indentations of a certain curved shape; its flat surface is internally subdivided by the veining and bears on its rich green a circle of greenish-brown, beginning at a little distance from the stem. In the same way the umbrella-shaped inflorescence with its corolla of buds and umbel of blossoms, the single blossom (best seen in profile) with calyx and heart-shaped petals, the form and pigmentation of the thicker stalks and secondary stalks can be analysed. Finally the whole plant is studied in its general tiered structure (Plate 16b).

Method

Modern art teaching has found that a child can make an ordered picture of anything of which he has a clear visual image that he can describe verbally. The character of this picture is of course determined by the child's individuality and stage of development. It must not be judged by naturalistic standards of accuracy. Artistic standards—unity, articulation, and organisation of colours and forms—on the other hand are applicable. The aim of our art teaching is to make them so. The success of a pictorial representation depends therefore on its being founded upon an inner imgage, not upon the simultaneous observation of the subject, which should only be studied again if it is necessary to revise or clarify an inadequate visual image. The inner image alone has the power to produce a pictorial unity, the essence of artistic creation. On the other hand, the purely external imitation of a subject is merely a sum of accidental and instantaneous impressions, which can never be fused into a whole. Only someone (the artist) who has achieved independence of the accidental can create in immediate confrontation with an external subject.

G 5 **Bunch of Lilac (12 upwards)**

> Painting in splashes of colour followed by brush drawing in poster colours. Drawing block, box of poster colours, brush.

This theme is also begun by study of the subject (as under G 4), but the less easily analysed structure of the lilac (grape-like growth of the flowers, bushiness of the leaves) demands a different approach and painting technique, especially if a bunch and not a single spray is to be painted. Whereas the geranium plant was conceived as an analysable structure of all its members (also possible with each individual spray of lilac and the combination of several sprays into a clearly articulated whole), we consider the lilac as a structure of *masses*. We are still concerned with the structural detail in a superficial sense, but, for the sake of painting it in a different way, we allow the tiered form of the whole structure to dominate our impression, the highest tier being the flowerhead, the middle one the bushy leaves, the bottom one the sheaf of stalks.

Method

We mix three different pools of colour on our palettes (lid of the paintbox) for the upper, middle and lower zones of the picture. For the flowerhead zone we need white poster paint mixed with various violet-reddish, bluish, brownish tints in several shades, from light to deep violet. The shape of the flowerhead is like that of an 'upright' or slightly inclined bunch of grapes. Without considering its separate flowerets for the moment, we paint its whole shape as one area of colour, distinguishing only its general gradation. The flowerheads may intersect occasionally. Below this relatively separate flower zone lies the central leaf zone of various shades of green, again left without any structural detail. Before we paint the final stem zone (which may be brush-drawn in structural detail from the first), an even, harmonious background colour is applied.

This underpainting of the large areas is followed by an opaque brush drawing of the structures in really thick colour. The

136

structures of the flowerheads are sketched with the brush (without any complete enclosing of small or large areas) in close clusters of starlike flowerets (light or dark, according to the shade of the underpainting), oversweeping and softening the sharp edges of the underpainted areas; the close-growing, sometimes overlapping leaves are sketched in the same way (dark greens for their contours) and, finally, whatever accentuations are needed to the structure of the stems.

Dead Nettle (12 upwards) G 6

> White resist painting (see *150 Techniques in Art*, p. 83). Drawing block, tube of white poster paint, sable brush, tin palette (i.e. lid of the paintbox), waterproof ink, large flat brush or fixative spray.

The plant is studied as under G 4 and 5. The chief feature of the dead nettle is that its flower (labiate) consists of two equal parts and can be represented equally characteristically from 'front' or the 'side' view. We choose the side view because it is the child's view (Plate 17 a).

Method

The process of resist begins with a brush drawing in poster or gouache white. We allow a very faintly drawn compositional sketch in pencil merely to indicate the main outlines of the whole plant and the relative position of its details, no more. For the careful brush drawing, we mix a little white on the palette to an opaque but not sticky consistency. We avoid any impressionistic vagueness of line; each line is to make a clear and definite statement (about the nature and veining of the leaves, the juncture of the stems, the nodes of growth, the structure and hairs of the stalk, etc.). When dry, the finished brush drawing is either overpainted with a large brush or sprayed (fixative spray) with waterproof ink. This too must dry completely before the parts covering the white lines are rubbed lightly with the hand under the tap. The clean sharp lines of the brush drawing now stand out clearly against the dark ground.

Further themes: Pinecones; Ferns; Dandelions; Plantains; Apple Blossom; Pine Twig; Corn Cob; Sunflowers; Thistle.

ANIMALS

G 7 Puppies Playing (10 upwards)

> Painting in poster colours. Drawing block, pencil, box of poster colours, sable brush.

Needing a living subject for my pupils to study I borrowed a friend's wire-haired terrier for a few hours and took her to school. The unexpected sight worked like magic. Everyone's powers of observation were concentrated without the slightest effort. Sweety wanted to settle down comfortably but it wasn't time for that yet. First she had to submit to searching study, standing on my desk. From her nose to the tip of her tail, from her ears to the pads of her paws we described and named her every feature. The general movements of her body were noted: for instance, the characteristic springy curve from the top of her forehead down her back. Sweety had to turn and twist, to stand on her hindlegs and to roll on her back because our theme was 'Puppies Playing' (Plate 17b).

Method

An adequate store of impressions in the visual memory is far easier to use in drawing than direct observation of the animal. Visual memories are adaptable, whereas a model must be copied from a fixed viewpoint. All artists discover this fact and we use the experience for teaching. While drawing is going on, the model disappears from his pedestal and gives place to the 'inner' model. A pencil sketch decides the approximate arrangement of the picture, so that the masses may be balanced, and shows the main lines and movements of the two (or more) animals. The painting is at first confined to the figures of the animals; a flat underpainting followed by overpainting of the modelling and structure suggest itself for the older pupils. The lines of the bodies can be revealed in the painting of the rough hair; the curves of the limbs can be shown by gradations of shading applied with opaque, thick colour either in broad strokes of the bristle brush, or fine lines with an almost dry sable brush. The background may either be left plain or filled.

138

Plate VI

Group of Houses (G 12), in poster colours, by a 17-year-old girl. Width 22 inches

Plate 17

Puppies Playing (G7), pen drawing, by a 14-year-old boy. Width 16 inches

b Dead Nettle (G6), resist painting, by a student teacher. Height 24 inches

c Frog hunting a Bluebottle (G8), in poster colours, by a 10-year-old boy. Width 24 inches

Plate 18

a Railway Bridge (G 10), pen drawing, by a 14-year-old boy. Width 24 inches

b Church (G11), in poster colours, by a 14-year-old boy. Height 24 inches

> Painting in poster colour with restricted palette. Drawing block, pencil, box of poster colours, brush.

What gives the first impulse to the choice of a subject? Is it the child's impulse of spontaneous interest in the content or the teacher's desire to use it for a particular pedagogic purpose? That this always remains a moot point shows that both motives must always be present. The basis of the art of teaching is the ability to reconcile the two demands in one lesson.

In order to have occasion for painting with a palette limited to shades of green, that is, to develop greater discrimination in the use of colour, I chose the theme 'A Frog in the Grass'. To make the lesson more fun, I let them watch a frog hunting a bluebottle. From 10 onwards, they start to study the animal's characteristic form (as under G 7); this study may be supplemented by use of a biological or a preserved specimen in the advanced classes. (Photographs can reveal much that may pass unnoticed in study from life. To obtain a three-dimensional visual image capable of movement it is essential to show several different photographs of the same animal so that the memory is not limited to one accidental view.)

Method

A frog, small as it is, is yet suited by its compact yet elastic body for the large central figure of a picture. True, this produces a giant frog, which could have some fairy tale justification but should in any case be accepted as an artistic reality.

A pencil drawing shows the organisation of the picture, the way the animal propels itself and its main characteristics. The green spots and stripes of its back and belly and their intersection by the blades of grass are drawn (Plate 17c). Painting can then begin. No preliminary practice in mixing various greens is needed. This abstract painting exercise is more beneficial if carried out through the concrete demands of the theme. A practice sheet of paper is useful for trying the effect of new mixtures of colour. The uninitiated pupil is always surprised not merely that green can be produced from two quite different colours, but that it need never lose its basic character whatever other colour is added to it, but thereby reveals its inexhaustible variety.

G 9 Spider and Web (8 upwards)

Various techniques: e.g. reverse print (see *150 Techniques in Art*, p. 60), plaster engraving (p. 39), embroidery on net or thread appliqué (p. 54), underglass engraving (p. 41), foil relief (p. 74), resist painting (p. 84), and many others.

One can either treat spider and web as equally important, or enlarge the insect to become the subject of the picture. In either case, we approach the theme essentially as a drawing one, examine the body of the spider in its minutest structures, and markings, the net with its delicate, centralised pattern, rhythmic stretch and miraculous weave. Possible additions are dew-drops shimmering on every thread, fine twigs on which the airy structure is suspended, a great bluebottle which easily breaks through the beautiful treacherous snare.

Method

Besides drawing with pencil, brush or pen, there are many printing techniques suitable for the young and easy to acquire, which awaken fresh interest through the fascination of a new medium. For these techniques, which are nearly all inexpensive, see *150 Techniques in Art*.

Further themes: Lizards and Salamanders; The Dovecote; Tropical Fish; The Nextdoor Cat; A Swarm of Bees; Large Grasshopper; Turkey; Geese; Family of Beetles; Caterpillar.

ARCHITECTURE

G 10 Railway Bridge (8 upwards)

Pen and ink drawing. Drawing block, penholder with drawing nib, waterproof ink.

Our towns and villages contain many structures and pieces of architecture which would be promising themes. If we develop an eye for such fruitful subjects it should be easy to open our pupil's eyes to their exciting possibilities.

A railway bridge in the centre of the city, surrounded by buildings of contrasting styles, can be translated by a child into a miracle of graphic ingenuity (Plate 18 a).

Intensive study of the subject must precede the work in

144

class. The complex impression can be analysed and held only by being put into words. It is best to make it a game in which the teacher joins, each one making his own observations and discoveries.

Method

The older the pupils, the more essential an initial composition sketch becomes. A generalised pencil drawing showing the relation of the masses will suffice; it should not include any detail. The definitive pen drawing makes use of the sketch, but can change and replan wherever it can be improved. The aim is to achieve a rich graphic rendering of the impressions gained of the subject from visual memory and creative fantasy. The essential help the teacher can give is fourfold: in remembering and recapitalating impressions, in encouraging pupils to enrich, decorate or draw structural detail, in the guidance of concentration from stage to stage, and in the pointing out of exemplary work.

Church (all ages)

G 11

> Painting in poster colours. Drawing block, pencil, box of poster colours, brush.

Every age-group approaches this theme differently. For the little ones everything is still unanalysed subjectivity; the older ones need analytical discussion to help them to bring details and characteristics to mind. Their work expresses these differences faithfully: first the naive drawings of children just starting school, subjective experience expressed in direct symbols; then the expressive attempts at realism of the middle school, which, though they all represent the same church, studied by the whole class until they knew it by heart, all make quite distinct individual statements; and, finally, the work of the upper school, either markedly objective or markedly individual.

Method

The drawing and painting of architecture is the task of translating the three-dimensional subject into the two-dimensional picture (Plate 18b). The question 'How?' must inevitably be asked at some point. Before the age of 10 and often until the beginning of adolescence, this question is not a critical one because man, at a pre-perspective stage, avoids the problem of three-dimensionality by naive 'fusion of the ontotropic' (this is how the process of non-perspective representation—which consists in the flattened combination of different foreshortened, 'good' views of a subject—has been described by Ehrenstein). From the age of 10 we begin to come to terms with the 'reality' of appearances, at first without critical inhibitions by means of experiments in parallel-, central- and vanishing-point perspective. Most people do not go beyond this stage and there is no pedagogic or artistic objection to its hybrid productions, since as expressions of a stage of development they are self-justified and since the question of realistic perspective cannot affect the artistic value of a drawing, which is independent of it. One may even assert, without arousing the opposition of the experts, the principle that, at all stages of artistic creation, a naive use of perspective leads to better artistic results than a constructively correct one.

G 12 **Group of Houses (16 upwards)**

> Painting in poster colours with bristle and sable brushes. Drawing block, pencil, box of poster colours, with tube of white, pointed sable brush, round bristle brush.

The first task is to find a good subject for our picture. Utrillo's pictures of houses and streets in Paris are of particularly well chosen subjects. In contrast with the conventional prettiness of souvenir postcard and bourgeois drawing-room pictures, a street scene, to be of any artistic value must be strong and austere in composition. Such subjects can, of course, be found not only in Paris, but in any part of the world, usually unnoticed just around the corner.

Method

My upper-school class are sitting and standing around me in front of a group of houses forming a corner, opposite the school (Colour Plate VI). We are making a rough sketch which we shall develop into the definitive painting from memory in the classroom. The object of the sketch is to decide the disposition of the buildings and their surroundings, pavement, front gardens and trees. Details, such as doors, windows, balconies, etc., are only faintly indicated. The child's habit of starting with a detail which he finishes off completely must therefore be overcome. To avoid slavish copying of the subject, the

146

detailed brush drawing (in black, dark blue, or possibly red, etc.) is not started until we are back in class. This sable-brush drawing is to carry the detail well forward, even though the final broad painting in stippled technique with the almost dry-bristle brush is going to blur much of it. This, the actual painting, will give separate relief to the main surfaces and details of the houses by means of well contrasted thickly opaque colour (thickened with white to gouache), until finally the whole picture, including the pavement and sky, is covered with paint. By this stage the picture should give a clear general idea of the subject. Contours, the sharpness and hardness of which have partly been lost in the course of the broad overpainting and hitherto neglected details of architecture or foliage can now be drawn with the sable brush.

Further themes: The Towers of our Town; We Visit the Cathedral; Building Site; Our Street Corner; Village Scene; The Market Square; The Gasworks; On the School Staircase; In the Station; Castle Ruins.

LANDSCAPE

Churchyard (15 upwards) G 13

> Painting in poster colours. Drawing block, box of poster colours, sable brush, possibly also bristle brush.

Pure landscape themes are scarcely suitable for the lower classes as young children have no interest in them. Without some guidance, the middle classes have a tendency to produce either conventionally schematised or formless pseudo-impressionistic landscape, because the scope of a landscape is beyond their creative range. It is therefore best at this stage to set only such individual landscape themes as have associations with experience or fantasy (see C 13 and 14, F 13, H 14). For the middle and upper grades, outdoor study as a preparation is possible. A combination of architecture and vegetation such as a churchyard makes the approach easier (Plate 19 a). The typical vegetation of a churchyard (yews and other evergreens) helps to simplify the painting process by its stark 'architectural' outlines.

Method

The trees and shrubs are studied exclusively in their characteristic outlines and first painted as areas of colour. Afterwards
their structure, also observed beforehand, is drawn with the
brush. For the sake of the composition, it is advisable to choose
close groups of overlapping trees and to avoid depth. Also in
the near foreground are the gravestones and crosses, separated
by short paths. The theme itself decides the choice of colour,
but we should attempt, by careful mixing of colours and by
avoiding pure colours or strong colour-contrasts, to achieve a
unity and harmony of colour. This does not mean that we must
renounce contrast of light and shade without which a picture
appears inarticulate. The overdrawing, which indicates structures and the relationship of surfaces, heightens the articulation
if a strong, dark colour is used. The formal representation of
the complex structure of the various trees which cannot be
copied in its infinite detail demands some formal inventiveness.

G 14 **Trees in Winter (16 upwards)**

> Pen drawing. Drawing block, penholder and drawing nib, water-
> proof ink or designer's colour, if necessary black ballpoint pen,
> felt pen, etc.

In late autumn, winter and early spring, the essential problems
of landscape are clearly revealed: the three elements of landscape are seen separately: the changing surface of the earth,
the atmospheric depths of the sky and the tree, representative
of all vegetative life.

For the upper school, the tree is the problem in landscape
painting simply because land and sky, important as they are,
do not enter man's artistic consciousness until a later stage.
Nevertheless a skilful teacher can give his pupils some groping
awareness of the whole landscape. The difficulties which unfold are best tackled by means of surface detail and attributes
(such as roads, fences, fields, clouds).

The theme 'Trees in Winter' means, in contrast to the foregoing theme, 'Churchyard', trees as analysed structures. The
filigree of a leafless tree can already be appreciated by children
as something strangely beautiful and living (Plate 19b). This
magical charm lies in the regular rhythm of their growth, which
flows from the trunk to the smallest twig. The rhythmic growth

of every kind of tree obeys a different law. We shall attempt to sense and to describe the rhythm of various trees by observing them closely. A further distinguishing characteristic of trees, is the pattern of their bark which consists either of circles or of vertical lines.

Method

With this store of mental images, we return to the classroom. If an extensive work is planned, it is advisable to go out of doors several times and there to study and to draw objects one at a time. (This concentration on separate portions of the task eases and enliven a large, lengthy picture, through the study and drawing of the fresh material continually introduced, and through the reconsideration of the composition in relation to the new elements to be incorporated.)

Just as the shape and substance of a great tree-trunk is revealed by its tangible surface structure, so the changing surface of the land is revealed by the shapes and surface structure of roads, of meadowland and rocky hollows. These too need to be studied out of doors. Thus our pupils begin the second task in the course of their drawing, standing on the grass under the trees and looking ever further afield.

Corner of the Garden (16 upwards)   G 15

> Felt pen or charcoal pencil drawing. Drawing block, charcoal pencil, felt pen or crayon-pencil, black, sepia.

Choice and presentation of the theme: enclosed sectors of landscape, in which the existing relationships sustain the composition, are the most suitable themes for drawing. A fenced corner of a garden with outbuildings and a gable of the house is an ideal theme. A tidy, well-kept front garden lacks interest, so a certain picturesque untidiness is also desirable to give greater diversity and movement to the picture. In contrast with this disorder, a few clear-cut elements should stand out: for example, the stout trunk of a pine, a stack of logs, the wall of the shed behind it and a piece of the fence. Now we have a clear, comprehensible theme for our felt-pen drawing.

Method

We may begin with a faint pencil sketch to determine the size and relationship of the elements in the picture, but none of the detail. The lines of the felt-pen drawing cannot be corrected,

149

so some practice sketches may be made on scrap paper. We practise drawing the subjects not by generalised, meaningless hatching but in relation to their shape and structure: for example the bark of a tree, the movement of a tuft of grass in front of the shed, the planks of which the shed is constructed and their graining, a little foliage, etc. When we have found a satisfactory 'graphology', in which to represent the manifold complexity of appearance in a simplified and condensed form, we can begin to build up the picture from the structures and contours of the objects. These should follow their inner construction, never precede it. As the picture is not to be painted, the variety of colour is replaced by the varying density and character of the objects portrayed in clear and distinct relation to one another.

Further themes: Piles of Logs; Edge of the Forest; In the Quarry; A Little Pinewood; Old Willows by the Stream; House in the Park; Allotments; View from the Window; View over Arable Land with Various Crops; An Avenue of Trees; Industrial Landscape.

IV PICTURE DICTATIONS

DICTATIONS FROM WORKS OF ART

Rousseau: 'Tropical Forest with Lion' (10 upwards)   H 1

Brush or wax crayon drawing followed by painting. Drawing block, box of poster colours and brush, or wax crayons.

I will explain my aim in dictating a picture from an original work of art or its reproduction. Through following and carrying out the picture as it is described, sentence by sentence, with his crayon or brush, the pupil acquires a working, creative contact with the artistic aim of the painter. It is almost impossible to imagine a more intensely constructive experience or a more direct physical involvement in the problems of a work of art especially since it is followed by study of the original picture or a reproduction. Experience has proved that this exercise makes pupils genuinely eager to look at the original work and incomparably more appreciative of its masterly solution of the artistic problems they have themselves experienced.

Method

Rousseau's picture of a 'Tropical Forest with Lion', like many of his paintings and other simply and clearly constructed pictures, is well suited for analysis into a picture dictation (Plate 19c).

When the main idea of the picture has been explained in a few words, the dictation is best begun with the placing in the picture area of the central figure or object or of the foreground objects in such a way that the subsequent building up of the picture in detail, either according to dictated positions or at the pupil's own discretion, is possible without danger of the picture going astray, i.e. losing its unity. There is no question of absolute obedience to a dictated pattern in either the planning or the completion of the picture, but rather of giving the pupil the opportunity to decide upon the best proportions and placing of his figures and the best relationship of lines and colours for his own composition. It is therefore equally possible either to

151

continue the dictation into a minute description of every
detail of the composition, or simply to mention the main objects in the picture and to leave their visualisation and arrangement entirely to the pupil.

H 2   **Santa Maria della Salute, Venice (14 upwards)**

> Lino cut (see *150 Techniques in Art,* p. 57). Drawing block, pencil,
> piece of lino, cutting tool, lino-printing ink, rubber roller, pane of
> glass, newspaper, absorbent paper for the print.

Large architectural monuments grew up slowly from their
foundations.

From the platform of its widespread steps rises the magnificent Baroque church of Santa Maria della Salute in Venice,
in a triple-tiered structure surmounted by cupola and lantern.
We shall build up our picture in the same way, from the
octagonal platform of the steps, via all the detail of columns
and porticos, upwards to encompass the whole structure. Each
pupil puts down each sentence of the dictation on his paper in
the form of a careful drawing. We always pause to allow the
slower pupils to catch up, so that the majority of the class is
following. During this pause those who have finished can im-
prove their work. When the dictation proceeds to a new stage,
what is still incomplete must be left, so that we all begin the
new stage together. Some time is left for catching up at the
end of the lesson.

Method

After these introductory hints on the theme and the method
of working, we begin by indicating the point in the picture
where the construction of the flight of steps is to be begun. At
the centre of the top step, stands a Romanesque arched door-
way and with this we begin the building itself. To right and
left the arch is flanked by two columns on high plinths. Their
capitals attain the same height as the arch. These four columns
support a heavy marble architrave (or beam) and the flat
Grecian tympanum (triangular gable) above it, the latter sur-
mounting the inner columns only. This whole structure (a
portico) forms one of the eight sides of the circular first tier of
the building. Two similar porticos are visible to right and left.
And so on . . . .

When the drawing is finished, it is transferred to the lino

and cut either for a white-line or a black-on-white print. For the cutting and printing processes see A9 and *150 Techniques in Art,* pp. 57-8.

Gauguin: 'Arearea' (12 upwards)

Painting in poster colours. Drawing block, pencil, box of poster colours, brush.

A picture dictation can sometimes take the following form: an intensive (or possibly only very brief) study of the painting precedes the dictation. This method aims to heighten the impression already gained of the painting by its subsequent active analysis in the dictation exercise. This exercise can, by a shift of emphasis, be developed into a kind of learning of the picture by heart, so that the teacher merely assists the pupil's memories during dictation; this exercise is rather similar to that of drawing after study of an object (see G1-15).

Method

Gauguin's 'Arearea' is one of his most beautiful South Sea paintings and is chosen for the clarity of its composition. The horizontal, oblong picture plane contains three points of concentration: (1) in the centre of the right half of the picture two girls sitting on the grass framed by the trunk and branch of a tree which is close to the righthand edge of the picture; (2) in the upper part of the left half of the picture: a group of small figures, consisting of three women worshipping an idol, who are arranged parallel with the edge of the picture; (3) at the bottom of the left half of the picture: a dog walking along the ground plane of the picture towards its centre. The rest of the plan of the picture is equally easy to remember and to dictate. There are scarcely any intersections.

'Arearea' means 'gaiety'. The warm, rich colours and the simple, lyrical mood of the picture—one of the girls is playing a flute, the other listening—captivate the beholder. The analytical exercise of painting this picture from visual memory, by means of a dictation, gives an unforgetable experience of Gauguin's art and of this masterpiece.

Further themes: Picasso: 'Pavilion on the Seashore'; Munch: 'The Deathbed'; Derain: 'Landscape with Church'; Utrillo: 'Church of St Margaret'; Notre Dame, Paris.

DICTATIONS FROM THE TEACHER'S MEMORY OF WORKS OF ART

H 4   **Cathedral Square, Pisa (14 upwards)**

> Resist painting (see *150 Techniques in Art*, p. 83). Drawing block, pencil, tube of white poster paint, sable brush, palette, drawing ink, large flat brush or fixative spray.

Just as a dictation can be 'read' from a picture in front of one (see H1-3), it can also be taken from one's visual memory of a work of art. A reproduction of a work that we know and that would be suitable for a picture dictation is not always to hand, but we have a vivid image of it in our mind's eye which we can communicate to others by a good description. Moreover a picture dictated from memory has the advantage of being stripped of all inessentials which simplifies the act of communication.

Method

Anyone who has gazed entranced on the Cathedral Square of Pisa, one of the most beautiful in the world, even if he is not lucky enough to have stood before that miracle in marble but has only a good photograph to rely on, cannot easily forget the perfect balance of its Romanesque architecture, its eternal repetition of the same noble forms, the splendid simplicity of its proportions (Plate 19 d).

The best picture dictations are inspired by our enthusiasm for a work of art. This enthusiasm enables us to experience the work as a whole and yet to notice its every detail with delight. These two abilities are the foundations of a good visual memory upon which a good memory dictation depends. The capacity to memorise is greatly increased if a careful check upon its accuracy is kept. In this way, the artistic experience of the teacher is itself enriched and deepened in the course of dictation and, by putting his own memories into words, he will come to understand more and more clearly in what way a picture should be described so that it may be experienced pictorially and in its true essence by someone else. He will also learn to avoid the pitfalls which beset such a passing on of experience and which may make it impossible for the impression to be received.

For the resist technique, see F9.

Painting in poster colours. Drawing block, pencil, box of poster colours, brush.

The picture develops in the memory gradually. First, the eye is drawn to the background of the horizontal edge of the picture, its little warehouses hidden. Signal masts point upwards and seawards. In the water in front of the jetty, on the left of the picture, are three little cargo-boats with tall funnels. As they are seen broadside on they overlap one another slightly, anchored side by side. On the left of the strip of beach, which also runs horizontally, parallel to the ground plane of the picture, two or three little boats are beached. The shore is protected from the sea only by a breakwater on the left edge of the picture.

Method

The description of these simple objects, of their starkly parallel, horizontal-and-vertical plan, and their clear position in the picture nevertheless produces in the mind of each hearer a totally different inner picture. Every human being's 'picture-thinking' is so completely personal that, however many people were to hear the same description, no two of them would either visualise or draw the same picture. It is good that it should be so and we respect the fact as a very important truth. The comparison of the results of a picture dictation is therefore at least as interesting as that of the results of other exercises. The differences between them are even greater than those between pictures based on impressions and study of external objects.

The 'Oude Kerk', Amsterdam (13 upwards)   H 6

Coloured brush drawing on tinted paper. Drawing block, box of poster colours, brush.

Many Gothic churches and cathedrals have a polygonal chancel with tall narrow lancet windows, richly decorated with elaborate tracery. The steep walls between these windows are supported from the outside by flying buttresses carried by arches. In mediaeval times little shopkeepers' stalls and tradesmen's booths often sheltered beside the high stone pediments of these chancel buttresses. One may still see today some survivals of this comfortable co-existence, for example, in Amsterdam, whose 'Oude Kerk', picturesquely situated beside one of the old canals, is still a vivid picture in my memory. Such a remembered view is very suitable for a picture dictation, because of its simple, clear construction.

Method

We begin by covering the whole background of our picture with freely rhythmic, broad expanses of colour. We intend to make a brush drawing in light and dark or in a contrasting colour on the already coloured background, in response to the dictation. The colour of the brush drawing is to change, wherever necessary, as it crosses a different expanse of background colour. Finally the various parts of the building will be brought into stronger contrast with one another and with the sky, possibly by the modification of the background colour.

The dictation begins with the stalls and booths in the foreground. The high, narrow, tiny huts can be described one by one, or else left to the pupils' own individual fantasy. Behind this row of little buildings, high into the middle of the picture and towards the top, rises the first tall lancet window. Some idea of the characteristics of Gothic architecture might well be woven into the dictation here. The designing of the second and third lancet windows can be entrusted to the pupils. Thus the building goes on, stage by stage.

Further themes: Temples of a Greek City;   The Colosseum, Rome; Chancel of a Norman Cathedral (Durham);   Front of a Gothic Cathedral (Wells);   Klee: 'Little Rhythmic Tree Landscape'; Marc: 'The Three Roan Horses';   Seurat: 'The Port';   Barth: 'Horse-Race'.

DICTATIONS FROM PHOTOGRAPHS

H 7   **Equestrian Statue in the Park (8 upwards)**

> Painting in poster colours. Drawing block, pencil, box of poster colours, brush.

Many photographs of striking monuments achieve an excellent picture by good placing and lighting. Such a monument may not always be a first-class work of art but it may, nevertheless, be an excellent theme for a drawing dictation. In a favourable position in the park of a little town, in the centre of a square

156

surrounded by buildings and stately trees, stands an equestrian statue on a pedestal several steps from the ground. Handsome iron railings protect it from intruders. A few passers-by, in their Sunday-best, pause to admire it casually.

Method

The whole photograph (a vertical oblong) is concentrated around the central pedestal on which the statue stands. The dictation of the preliminary pencil sketch starts with the statue. First the pedestal is described in detail, and, once it is erected, the bronze statue itself is set up. It is flanked by young trees with delicate foliage and transparent tops which are lower than it. At the four corners of the steps are small stone posts supporting an elaborately wrought-iron railing. Whether we draw first the railing, or the figures in front of or behind it, is not important. Some intersection always occurs when one adds to the foreground at the end of a composition. We can rub out the pencil lines of the parts to be hidden.

In painting we must remember that delicate details, with many small projections, must not be painted until we have decided whether the background is to be painted or plain.

The Wupper Valley Suspension Railway (12 upwards)   H 8

> Pen drawing. Drawing block, penholder and drawing nib, drawing ink or designer's colour.

Many subjects make more effective drawings than paintings. The iron girders, the supporting framework of the suspension railway invite a pen drawing. An indelible pen and ink drawing requires a carefully considered sequence of dictation. In the representation of objects at considerable distance from one another, it is best to start with the foreground objects in order to avoid intersections.

Method

The structure supporting the Wupper Valley suspension railway follows the narrow bends of the little river, which flows through the town to join the Wupper, and above which the strange hanging tracks of the railway and its 'stations' are built. One after another, the trains race from station to station, hanging on their wheels, slanting round the curves, cutting across the bridges of the river, disappearing and reappearing under the great railway bridges which, in their turn span, the

157

whole network. This traffic network in all its mobility and complexity is enclosed on all sides by the buildings of the town so that not an inch of space is left free. It presents a characteristic aspect of the period of early industrial development which today has a picturesquely chaotic fascination. As the dictation proceeds, our postcard photographs serve to keep clear in our minds the typical parts of the scene which are being translated by our pupils into miracles of graphic ingenuity. The chaotic scene comes under our control as though by the power of magnetism, but in fact everything depends upon the method of dictation. We must begin with a careful description of the structures in the foreground, and guide one stage after another to completion, so that each new addition is clearly related to all that preceded it.

H 9 Corner of an Old Village (14 upwards)

> Direct painting in poster colours. Drawing block, box of poster colours, brush.

We deliberately choose a photograph which presents many problems of perspective. We intend to demonstrate that visual relationships such as foreshortening of lines and narrowing of angles need be no impediment in dictation. The pupil's visual images of objects described in dictation are usually without perspective. The combination of such a-perspective elements in a picture is in no way detrimental to the result. On the contrary, if all the objects in the picture appear conceptually in their pre-perspective 'good' view, the best common denominator has been found under which the picture can achieve unity.

Method

After a short explanation of the intended picture, the first stages of the direct uncorrectable painting are dictated; they are single objects such as the facade of a house, an archway, a fence—the positions of which largely determine how the picture area is to be used (Plate 20 a). Some pictures will already be more filled than others, so that some of the objects in the dictation have to be left out; it does not matter if others still have gaps in their composition when the dictation is finished. They can complete their pictures from their own imagination. At the start of the painting either the choice of colours is left

Plate 19

*a Churchyard (G13), in
poster colours, by an
18-year-old girl*

*b Trees in Winter (G14),
pen drawing, by a
16-year-old girl*

*c Tropical Forest with
Lion (H1), in poster colours,
by a student teacher*

*d The Cathedral Square,
Pisa (H4), resist painting,
by a 16-year-old girl*

All 22 inches wide

Plate 20

a Corner of an Old Village (H9), in poster colours, by a student teacher. Width 22 inches

b Little Italian Port (H10), lino cut, by a student teacher. Width 17 inches

c The Prince Emil Gardens (H12), in poster colours, by a 13-year-old boy. Width 23 inches

Plate 21

*a   Building a Church (H13), in natural colours, by a 12-year-old girl.
Width 21 inches*

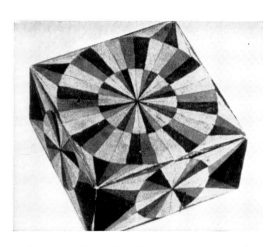

*b   Decorated Paper Box (J1), by a student teacher.
5½ x 5½ x 2¾ inches*

*c   Houses on the Mountainside (J5),
in poster colours, by a 12-year-old
girl. Height 22 inches*

Plate 22

a   Bridges and Men (J7), stencil picture, by a student teacher. Width 22 inches

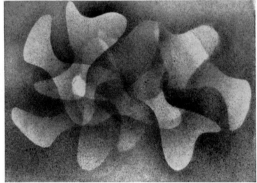

b   Form transparently stencilled (J13), spray print, by a student teacher. Width 24 inches

c   Cathedral (K9), isometric drawing, by a student teacher. Height 24 inches

free or the use of a limited range of colours (e.g. shades of brown and blue, modified with black and white) is agreed on.

Further themes: An Old Brickworks; Street Scene; Industrial District; Wharf with Cranes; View of City; Fountains with Sculpture; Market-Place with Half-Timbered Houses; Airport; Skeleton of a Mammoth in a Museum.

DICTATIONS OF SCENES REMEMBERED BY THE TEACHER

Little Italian Port (14 upwards)   H 10

> Lino cut (see *150 Techniques in Art*, p. 57). Drawing block, pencil, piece of lino, cutting tool, printing ink, rubber roller, small pane of glass, absorbent paper, newspaper.

The impression that the picturesque appearance of a little Italian port makes upon the spectator's memory rests upon the combination of a few characteristic features, which can easily be described for a dictation exercise. Thus the teacher's instructions could be to compose a picture of such a port from the following objects: three fishing boats in a small harbour bay, a bridge, on the shore about five tall, narrow houses with flat facades and closed shutters, a few palms or cypresses, mountain peaks in the distance.

Method

The composition of the picture and the shaping of the objects in detail is left to the pupils. The task set to the whole class demands an entirely personal translation of the given theme into a well-composed picture.

It should be noted that this form of dictation, in which all the material of the picture is given as part of the initial instructions (in contrast with the method of drawing out the instructions over the entire art period), reveals again how closely the principle of 'dictation' is linked with the advice normally given to the class on any exercise undertaken. In the last analysis, all exercises which are in some degree controlled are dictations; this fact should be kept in mind as well as the fact that the pupil's freedom of creation neither should nor can be curtailed by a picture dictation.

(For the lino-cutting technique see A 9).

163

H 11 The Painter in His Studio (10 upwards)

Painting in poster colours. Drawing block, pencil, box of poster colours, brush.

Themes with figures can also be dictated, though less frequently. Figures in movement are more difficult to grasp and describe than motionless objects. Our theme is comparatively simple since the painter has a characteristic pose in front of his canvas and the rest of the picture consists of motionless objects, the pictures covering or leaning against the walls of the studio. These finished canvases give us an opportunity of painting many more little picture dictations by the way, not to mention the half-finished or almost complete picture on the easel.

Method

This theme reveals again what a picture dictation really is. Whether I set an ordinary nature theme such as 'A Vase of Flowers', or frame a picture of a vase of flowers and hang it, as part of the dictation, in the painter's studio; or whether I introduce an imaginary figure of my own into a picture of 'The Fair' that the class is painting from their own visual memory, or hang a portrait in an empty space on the studio wall, there is no fundamental difference in my method of teaching. Dictation is involved in every case, even if it is not so called. A difference arises only when the choice and treatment of the theme is either left to the pupil or becomes free, through the withdrawal of the teacher's guidance. Even this distinction however is not absolute in the case of a picture dictation, since the given form demands an individual interpretation. Moreover nearly all the kinds of dictation recommended here allow essential freedom in the choice of composition, colour and form.

H 12 The Prince Emil Gardens (10 upwards)

Coloured brush drawing followed by painting in poster colours. Drawing block, box of poster colours, brush.

The labourers and gardeners who carried out the designer's instructions for the reconstruction of the public garden near the school, which had been destroyed in the war, probably went to work in much the same way as the 40 second-form girls who followed my picture dictation. Of course it took them

164

longer to lay down real paths and to plant real bushes and trees than to paint them. Today real couples can stroll through the Prince Emil Gardens, while our 'Prince Emil Gardens' decorates the school and many of the children's homes.

Method

We start in the top quarter of the picture space with the line of the hill-top on which the little palace still stands, just as it did before the war (Plate 20c). The main path climbs diagonally across the picture in gentle curves from right to left. From it branch winding side-paths dividing the rest of the garden diagonally. We include a small circular space with a fountain in our design. Now the first trees can be planted; subsequent ones must be carefully placed, followed by a few bushes to give decorative variety. At length, the park is laid out and the first visitors can enter; the architect and his wife naturally lead the procession. Now that we have planned everything, we can draw the outlines with pointed sable brushes. The final filling-in with paint of the delicately drawn coloured framework of the picture should not hide its lines but enhance their effect.

Further themes: Bridges; Railway Shunting Yard; A Stage; Skyscrapers; Exhibition of Veteran Cars; Open-air Exhibition of Sculpture; Landscape with Trees; Lumber Yard with Sawmill.

DICTATIONS FROM
THE TEACHER'S VISUAL IMAGINATION

Building a Church (11 upwards)   H 13

> Pen drawing tinted with natural colours. Drawing block, penholder and drawing nib, waterproof ink or designer's colour, natural colours, see below, brush.

The teacher's pictorial imagination is an inexhaustible source of themes. In his mind's eye he beholds imaginary landscapes with fantastic vegetation or architecture and the most varied scenes with figures. He feels for the right words to convey these imaginative creations and to enable them to be realised pictorially.

165

Method

'All the preparations have been made for the building of the church. Soon the foundations will be laid. Little by little they are growing before my eyes.'

It is interesting to see this happen in a picture, but in a different way and in a rather different sequence (Plate 21 a). We lay out our paper horizontally. On the bottom left side we place a round barrel, made of wooden staves, encircled by iron hoops. We can just see into the top of it. One pace to the right stands another just like it. Directly behind them both, almost touching them but slightly hidden by them, stand two more barrels. They are filled with sand in which tall wooden poles are planted, intersecting the top edge of the picture. These are to be the uprights of two scaffolding ladders, so we put rounded rungs between them. At about a man's height from the ground we insert a strong cross-plank, which is already a little curved under the weight of the builder's labourer whom we are going to put on it. Above the heads of the builders, who are still getting ready for work, a further plank stretches from ladder to ladder. The rest of the objects in the foreground are dictated in the same way, including the heap of sand which lies in front of the cement-mixer. Then the first workers are added. One shovels sand, while others stand working on the scaffolding or sit eating their sandwiches. The architect appears in consultation with the vicar. Behind all this finally appears the incomplete building itself, a wall with the arch of a door and a half-finished round window. The pendrawing is to be tinted with transparent 'natural' colours of our own manufacture and invention. Coffee produces a fine brown, spinach a useful green, boiled rose petals a reddish tint. This starts a competition. Who can find the most interesting raw materials for more colours?

H 14 **Circus Performers (8 upwards)**

> Painting in poster colours. Drawing block, pencil, box of poster colours, brush.

Dictation themes full of figures are left extremely free; the choice of attitudes and movements is largely left to the pupil. We have already indicated under H1, 3 and 10 that a picture dictation can allow varying degrees of freedom, right up to the point when it becomes no more than an introductory stimulus to the work, the mere giving of a title, and that it thus merges, without any break in continuity, with ordinary exercises in free composition, for which only the theme is given and which would in no way be considered as dictations.

Method

We start by drawing the circus ring. Pairs of beautifully caparisoned thoroughbred horses gallop into it and round and round it. Upon each horse stands an acrobat dressed in tights. Riding side by side, each pair of acrobats carries a slender girl who balances upon their shoulders, arms extended. So the strange and splendid procession circles the ring. In the background, perhaps even in front and on each side of the picture, sit the onlookers, on benches, above which, if the picture space allows, the top of the circus tent can be seen.

The solution of the spatial and anatomical problems of such a picture may safely be left to the varied resources of the different age-groups. The less we associate the theme with the restrictions and standards of perspective and anatomical 'rightness', the more 'rightly' it will develop in the artistic sense of the word. Each stage of artistic development finds its own solutions. For that very reason, we choose a free dictation, so that no restrictive demands (such as that the horses should be drawn either front-view or in half-profile) need inhibit the drawing.

Surrealist Ruins and Sculptural Remains (16 upwards)   H 15

> Wax engraving (see *150 Techniques in Art*, p. 36). Drawing block, wax crayons, possibly waterproof ink, engraving tool (e.g. pen-knife, nail-file or nail).

Romanticism and Surrealism are styles of art in which ruins play an important part. Whereas Romantic art dwelt upon the ruins of antiquity and of mediaeval romance, Surrealism was haunted by the symbols of impending catastrophe. Our world has become a world of ruins, warnings of men's boundless destructiveness which lie before the eyes of every child. May we never forget them amid the lofty post-war buildings of mushroom growth.

Method

We cover the entire surface of the paper with a thick background of bright wax colours (including blue). The colours may alternate in free rhythmic sequence (i.e. in well-related groups). When no paper is visible even between the lines of the hatching, we put on either a second, dark layer of wax (brown or black) or, to save trouble, a coat of waterproof ink or black powder paint with a size base. Now we have a 'night'-coloured layer on which the lines and shapes of the dictated drawing can be engraved with a penknife. The dictation begins with the tufts of grass and tall weeds in the foreground whence rise the brick walls of the nearest ruins. The chaotic pile of sculptural remains may be surrealistically treated. Everywhere growing things spring up against the night sky from the tall ruins. The shells of the buildings and monuments glow with ghostly colours.

Further themes: City of Temples; Interior of a Fantastic Church; An Engineroom; Old Mississippi Paddle Steamer; Large Industrial Constructions; The Snow-Princess on the Icebird; Workers Repairing High-tension Cables; Fashion Designer's Studio; Visiting a Hothouse.

V DECORATIVE ABSTRACT THEMES

APPLIED DECORATION

Folded Paper Box—Wax Sgraffito (8 upwards) J 1

> Stiff paper, scissors, wax crayons, scratching tool (e.g. penknife, nail-file, etc.) (see *150 Techniques in Art*, p. 37).

The outer and inner surfaces of a small cardboard box are to be decorated with a simple geometric engraved pattern of lines and shapes (Plate 21 b). For the technique see under B 12.

Method

A square piece of stiff paper is marked with a pencil dot in the centre. We now fold the corners back exactly to the centre. The folded corners are again folded in the same way, to the centre, so that they are halved. When we open them again, we find, in the centre of the large base, a small square with folded edges, which is to be the base or cover of the folded box. The long lines of two opposite sides of the small square are cut with the scissors to the edge of the paper. We now have two narrow and two wide folded parts round the centre square. Now begins the folding of the box, with the two wider folded parts. The corners are first folded to the middle and then folded double. Two narrow side-pieces of the box can now be bent up at right angles; the sides of their triangles are bent round towards the two sides of the box. Finally the two narrow sides can be raised and folded in the same way, so that the finished box is firmly bound together. The whole process is now repeated with a slightly larger or smaller square of paper for the top or base of the box.

Engraved Plaster Tile (8 upwards) J 2

> Plaster of Paris, mould (soup-plate, old tin, etc.), coloured ink, engraving tool (see *150 Techniques in Art*, p. 39).

Plaster and water in equal parts are stirred together and poured into a temporary mould, the bottom of which is covered with a pane of glass or piece of lino. The tile which results will become an engraving plate when covered with

169

black ink or paint. An engraving tool, such as a penknife, nail-file, etc., easily produces snow-white lines on the dark ground.

Method

Engraving a blackened tile with white lines and areas is a matter of decorative thinking and creation. All engraving, even when it represents nature, must disregard depth and perspective. In other words, all the elements of the design must be in the foreground. The flatness which we take for granted in abstract geometrical decorative forms is thus also required of an engraving of a 'Basket of Flowers'. The flowers growing in the woven basket are ranged side by side without any intersection. The decorative effect of such a subject can also be heightened by symmetrical arrangement, rhythmic repetition of identical or similar forms, and flat treatment of the entire picture plane. A certain archaic stiffness in children's style of drawing exactly answers this decorative purpose. The subjects below, all favourites of peasant art, with which our pupils' work has a certain affinity, are proven decorative figure—and object—themes.

Further themes: Bird; Cock; Fishes; Horse and Rider; Garland of Flowers; Cat; Lion; Stag; Fantastic Flower; Peasant Woman; Fabulous Beast; Enchanted Castle; Dragon; Swan; Mask; Angel, etc.

J 3   **Embroidered Wallhanging (all ages)**

> Various grounds are possible—hessian, net, calico, linen, etc.— and various threads—wool, worsted, remains of fabric, etc.; darning needle.

The style of embroidery depends on the materials and kind of decoration intended; the stitch may be satin-stitch, cross-stitch, stem-stitch, feather-stitch, etc. A simple in-and-out stitch may be used for linear patterns if the lines are continuous and enclose the design. An economical technique for filling up spaces can be developed from satin-stitch if the stitches are placed about an eight-of-an-inch apart and kept on the right side of the material only.

Method

Many children's drawings contain delightful incidental detail which would be ideal for translation into embroidery. Even some of the naive drawings done in the kindergarten are so vivid and expressive that commercial artists are glad to exploit them for purposes quite alien to their spirit. How much better employed they would be as decorative designs for the kindergarten and school. We stretch a piece of hessian on a large improvised wooden frame with drawing pins. Quite a number of children can then sit round it, resting it on their knees as they work. The general outlines of the figures are drawn with blackboard chalks to form one composition suitable for a wall decoration. Now the communal work can begin. Lest the children tire of it, they take turns at embroidering. General rules as to the size of the stitches and use of the thread are followed so that the style of the communal work may not be interrupted. A gaily coloured, carefully made design gradually develops.

Further decorative techniques: Paste Paper *(150 Techniques in Art,* p. 85); Fabric Painting (p. 81); Fabric Printing (p. 59); Cloth Batik (p. 81); Paper Batik (p. 80); Fabric Appliqué (p. 52); Transparent Glass Mosaic (p. 49); Painting Bowls, Vases, etc. (p. 87); Painting Matchboxes, etc. (p. 84); Easter Eggs (p. 84).

DECORATIVE CONVENTIONS: DECORATIVE TREATMENT OF REAL OBJECTS

Continuous Line Drawing: Ships (10 upwards) J 4

> Brush drawing and decorative painting of outlined shapes. Drawing block, box of poster colours, brush.

When special rules of the game are introduced for a particular exercise, in decorative transformation, pupils experience a delightful artistic process through which they discover the autonomous nature of artistic creation. This autonomy is based on the fact that art creates a new reality which is, as it were, independent of the reality of ordinary appearances. By means of the rules of the game, this autonomy, which is always present, is made conscious in the guise of a transparent code.

Method

We want to make a little fleet of miniature paddlesteamers into a decorative theme. Our rule is that everything in the picture, the whole shape of each ship with its bridge, funnel, etc., is to be expressed in a single flowing, moving line. Besides the hull, with its paddle-wheel and port-holes, a steamer has a funnel, a bridge, a cabin, a passengers' saloon with windows, and in the stern an open passenger deck. The continuous line style is to be clear and obvious. There will therefore have to be many turnings and curvings in it, in definite contrast with an ordinary drawing, which is composed by the addition of successive lines and not by means of one single curving line.

The transformation is most successfully achieved if the flow of the single line does not attempt to give a faithful copy of the subject drawn, but is allowed to develop a harmonious and lively rhythm of independent life and used to produce a well-balanced division of the picture plane. In order not to detract from the effect of the continuous line, the colour is kept at a certain distance from it.

J 5 Picture Based on a Convention: Houses on the Mountainside (10 upwards)

Drawing of the painting. Drawing block, pencil, box of poster colours, brush.

The stricter the rules of the game (see J4), the greater the similarity of the resulting pictures, and the less apparent the differences of age. Herein lies the drawback of game-convention themes. Used with due discretion, such techniques enable the pupil to exercise his right to independent creation of conventional abstract design. Their long-term aim is to enable him to discover his own abstract disciplines: that is, to invent his own conventions, which will give his creations a genuinely individual style.

Method

The following is a typical example of the use of a strict convention. We use the paper vertically. In free hand we draw horizontal and vertical pencil lines various distances apart across the paper. We then draw similar diagonal parallels in both directions. Now we find a medium-sized triangle, with the right-angle uppermost, in the centre of the picture; the triangle is traversed by a few vertical and horizontal, and even a few diagonal, lines. We paint the small sections of which this tri-

172

angle is composed in reddish shades. The shades can include mixtures of other colours, with red as well as light and dark red. Next further triangles are found at some distance from the first and similarly painted in variants of red. When there are enough coloured triangles in the picture, we consider them to represent the roofs of houses belonging to a village on the mountainside (Plate 21 c). We start by painting the walls of the lowest house, again using variations on a main colour. The colouring of the rest of the houses follows, always so that the base of the house disappears 'behind' the nearer houses. The parts of the picture left plain become the sky and the mountain, and are coloured as a foil to the houses.

Print with Folded Cardboard Stamp: Windmills (12 upwards)   J 6

> Drawing block, thin cardboard (old postcard), box of poster colours, brush.

Many a game-convention (see J 4 and 5) results directly from the tool or medium used. Such exercises are known as 'experiments with a medium'. They might equally well be called 'experiments with a tool', since the tool has also a determinant role. Many tools of art exist beside the usual pencil, brush and pen. When a piece of thin cardboard has been folded over and over, the firm ridge can be used as a printing stamp.

Method

According to the length of the cardboard stamp or the amount of paint which has been brushed on to it, straight or curved lines of various lengths can be printed. By using one stamp again and again, the imprint can be made fainter and fainter. These are the conventions according to which the game is to be played, to which the theme of the picture has to be adapted and through which its decorative transformation into a printed abstract design is achieved. A good artist will exploit the peculiarities of the medium to the advantage of the picture. He will be guided by the sharp-edged stamp into using clear-cut forms. The fixed length of the lines will not hinder him; he can use it to carry many of the outlines and inner lines of the objects beyond those objects themselves without blurring their outlines. He will use the multiple structure of the imprint to give multiple contour and structure to the objects in his picture and the gradual fading of the imprint to impart

173

gradations of tone. At the same time, he will avoid any arbitrary, undisciplined departure from the dynamic movement of the multiple lines of his composition, for he senses that every medium has also its dangers and that it is necessary to keep within certain limits which the picture dictates. The dynamic movement of a picture depends upon the harmony of its lines of direction.

Further themes: A Thread Picture: Herd of Giraffes; Paper Streamer Appliqué: A Schooner; Cross-stitch on Fine Canvas: Little Men and Women; Potato print: Red and Blue Horsemen; Black Silhouette Drawing: Occupations of our Family (divided by decorative frame); Forest-floor Mosaic with natural materials: Monster; Paper strip Appliqué: Towers and Bridges; Blot technique: Flying Demon; Rubbing of various Surfaces: Ferns and Grass; Ragged-paper Montage: Red Indians with Headdresses.

RHYTHMO-DYNAMIC COMPOSITION

J 7   **Stencilled Picture: Bridges and Men (14 upwards)**

> Stencil from stiff paper, scissors, pencil, box of poster colours, brush, drawing block.

The rhythmic recurrence of identical or similar elements is better than a variety of disconnected elements. This truth is demonstrated among other things by the following exercises in composition with stencils.

Method

We draw a simple bridge on the stiff paper and cut it out. Next we draw and cut out the figure of a man. Any simple drawing can be used, but the stronger the drawing, the stronger the effect achieved in the final composition. Whether it is a static figure or a dynamic figure, full of movement will decide the static or dynamic character of the picture. Either style can be effective in its way.

The one bridge and man are stencilled many times on a fresh sheet of paper. The quality of the final picture depends to a great extent on the placing of the objects, the balance of the masses, the vitality of the grouping and the use or avoidance of overlapping. A kind of expressionist décor is evolved (Plate

174

22 a). In the theatre everything is possible. Massed figures on bridges raise their arms seeming to threaten from above those on the bridges below who in turn threaten ... The strictness of the forms calls for a like strictness of colour.

Cardboard Rubbing: Ballet (15 upwards) J 8

Strong drawing paper or thin cardboard, scissors, pencil, drawing block, wax crayons or graphic pencil.

A stencil cut from stiff paper can easily be used as the object of a wax crayon rubbing. The stencil is laid under a fairly thin sheet of paper and rubbed with a crayon rolled horizontally. The contours stand out quite sharply even if the stencil is quite thin. (The process is similar to that of the rubbing 'Ferns and Grasses', J 4).

Method

One or two dancing figures are drawn and cut out. We try to achieve a clear and expressive silhouette in the drawing and avoid the clumsy intersections of the limbs with the body, which arise if we thought only in terms of ordinary drawing. Everyone can easily visualise that a ballet is far more effective when all the dancers make the same movement than when each dancer moves in his own way. This idea leads us to our cardboard rubbing 'Ballet'. The cut-out figures provide the elements from which two groups, dancing towards one another, can be composed. We achieve a good rhythmic composition by playing about with them. The rubbing process allows us to give gradations of the same colour by rubbing harder or more gently. It is also possible to make the figures overlap if the rubbing is interrupted at the parts to be hidden to avoid a double outline.

Spray Print: Wolfpack (all ages) J 9

Absorbent paper, scissors, pins, small hammer, waterproof ink or colour, fixative spray, drawing block, or scrap paper (lining paper, etc.). Group work.

The work is planned as follows. When the measurements have been decided each pupil cuts out the figure of a leaping wolf from his paper. The figures are then grouped into a suitable composition on the large sheet of absorbent paper and pinned

175

lightly but securely in their final positions. The sheet is then sprayed with ink, and, when it is dry and the stencils have been removed, the white-on-black spray print is finished.

Method

In cutting out the silhouettes we are careful to show all four legs separately. There is no need for a preliminary sketch. In order to keep to the agreed proportions, the sheets of paper can all be cut to size. In composing the figures on the background, we try to achieve the most varied grouping. The advantage of composing a picture with movable components is here specially obvious. Each group of children can demonstrate their own idea for a composition. Trying out ideas and abandoning them for better ones give the imagination new horizons. The best composition will be chosen, but we could make several spray prints from the same figures and then compare them.

Further themes: Dance of the Flamingoes; A Swarm of Locusts; Horses in a Paddock; Swarm of Bees; A Fir Plantation; Wooden Fences; Organ Pipes; Spiders; A Small Flotilla.

ABSTRACT TREATMENT OF OBJECTS

J 10   **Machine Forms (14 upwards)**

Resist painting (see *150 Techniques in Art,* p. 83). Drawing block, pencil, box of poster colours, brush, waterproof ink, large flat brush or fixative spray.

Instead of real objects, the idea of a certain category of object can be the theme of a picture, e.g. instead of a particular machine, the idea of a machine; instead of a particular cathedral, the idea of cathedrals. This is our approach to the abstract composition which is the aim of the lesson.

Method

A pupil of 14 guesses from the title 'Machines' that the picture is to be about the general nature of all machines. Revolving wheels, one behind another, conveyor belts and levers appear before his inner eye. There would be no real purpose in our designing a machine which, if made, would really work. The unlimited freedom to combine and construct, afforded by the idea of 'machines', has a specific pictorial purpose: what we are going to invent need not be effective in the technical sense,

176

but must be so in the pictorial sense. The structural validity and unity of the picture is for the eye alone. The eye demands unity of the picture: that is to say, a harmonious disposition of the masses within the given plane, a measured rhythm of forms and lines, a balanced reconciliation of the colour variations —and this demand sets the limits of our freedom.

We paint all the objects in the picture, but not the background, in strong poster colours. The resist technique consists in covering the whole picture with ink applied with a large brush or a fixative spray. The ink is absorbed only by the parts of the paper which are unpainted and can be washed off the painted parts under the tap, leaving them sharply outlined.

Plant Forms (15 upwards) J 11

> Painting in a limited range of poster colours. Drawing block, box of poster colours, brush.

The vegetable world contains an inexhaustible variety of forms. The young feel a spontaneous desire to look with reverence and awe on nature's multifarious beauty. The miracle of life is revealed to them through the mysterious power of nature to reflect the mind of a Creator.

The law of art, however, is that the ordered repetition of forms is better than their unlimited variation. Nevertheless the artistically and intellectually gifted pupils often tend to take complexity for beauty and the variety of their invention for art. Our task therefore is to train these gifted pupils to control their capricious overinventiveness.

Method

We must now put these theories into practice. In order to demonstrate clearly what we mean, we allow them to invent first two, or at most three, different plant forms (leaf or flower forms). We take these basic forms as the elements of our picture, which is to be built up from their rhythmic recurrence. It is organised therefore either in freely rhythmic groupings or separate bushlike structures, the masses of which are placed in dynamic relationship to one another. To enliven the theme, pairs of 'friends' from the plant world might possibly be combined.

The organisation of the colour also requires considerable

177

concentration. Our palette of shades of green (or of some other monochrome tonalities) cannot unite the detail into a significant pattern unless the changes of colour are strictly dictated by the rhythmic relationship of the elements, so that, for instance, all the lanceolate leaves are modulated to light green towards their tips.

J 12 Staircase Forms (16 upwards)

Grisaille painting. Drawing block, pencil, box of poster colours with tube of white, sable brush.

The setting of a theme with scaffolding, ladders, steps, or staircase forms as the motif, like all similar abstract composition exercises, allows the pupils either to abstract the given forms more and more for the sake of the formal unity of the design, or to play some game invented by the teacher such as 'construct a building consisting entirely of staircases'. Either method can be used according to the age and ability of the class. The teacher's aim is achieved through either: since it is to free the pupils from preoccupation with the subject matter through a gradual transition to thinking of the picture in terms of its formal qualities.

Method

A staircase can be represented in a two-dimensional, graphic or a three-dimensional, solid way, in a subjective, aperspective or in a constructional or constructivist way. All these styles are possible. Each individual version is right and can form the basis of a meaningful design. The task is to use this basic form to the best advantage as the unit of construction. It will produce a system of lines and planes which must all be related if the picture is to be a harmonious whole.

The single unit of form will be matched by unity of colour. In so-called 'grisaille' or painting in greys, all the tones from black to white are used, preferably by mixing black and white poster colours. The contrasting of the adjoining planes or receding surfaces must not be left to chance. A general scheme is needed and will, of course, vary from picture to picture.

Further themes: House Forms; Cathedrals; Snow-Crystals; Eyes; Animals; Dance of the Windows; Villages; Main Road and Side Roads (Klee); Roofs and Gables.

Plate 23

a   Texture of Lines (J15), measured drawing in pencil, by an 18-year-old girl. Width 24 inches

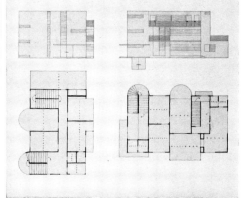

b   Design for a House (K2), ground plan and elevations, by a 17-year-old boy.

c   Surrealist Room (K10), in poster colours, by an 18-year-old girl. Width 22 inches

Plate 24

a   Romanesque Church (K13), scale model, by an 18-year-old boy

b   A Painter's House (K14), design model, by an art student

ABSTRACT CREATION

Form Transparently Stencilled (15 upwards) J 13

Spray print. Stiff absorbent paper, scissors, drawing block, pins, waterproof ink, fixative spray.

The technique in this exercise is the same as in other stencilled pictures (see J 8 and 9) but here the stencil form is completely abstract.

Method

An abstract form, like a real form, is only to be taken seriously as an artistic form if it is 'created', that is, full and complete in itself. An 'uncreated' and ill-proportioned form can be recognised immediately as such, whether it is meant to represent a real object or not. The design of an abstract form is therefore a genuine achievement which depends upon a sensitive feeling for quality. This sensitivity, though often undeveloped, is universal.

The cut-out form is attached to the background with pins and lightly sprayed with ink. This process is repeated in other positions on the background; overlapping of the forms can be tried, until a rhythm of darker and lighter planes is evolved (Plate 22b). According to the strength or delicacy of the colour, we achieve a more or less marked rhythmic alternation of light and dark tones, in which the original unit of form appears with varying distinctness. The capacity to visualise and achieve a pictorial effect can be developed by means of this stencil spray-print technique.

Floating Symbols (15 upwards) J 14

Rubbing of variously textured materials. Drawing block, scissors, variously textured materials, graphite pencil or wax crayon.

Even numbers and letters are conceived as forms in our mind's eye, and thus take on the character of objects. For this theme the pupils must therefore find symbols, which are not already fixed as visual forms, and endow them with forms. At the same time we must be on our guard against a juxtaposition of vague unrelated shapes and make disciplined clarity and simplicity our aim. For even an abstract symbol can be strong or weak, true or artificial, fundamental or superficial in character.

Method

We cut the symbols out of various materials of different surface quality. We can use fabrics or wallpaper, wire-netting or variously grained pieces of wood. The finding of suitable materials is a valuable exercise in itself. The pieces of material, laid under the paper and rubbed firmly with the crayon (rolled horizontally) produce a print-like result of delightful surface variations. It is not always necessary to cut the materials to special shapes. The forms of the symbols can be drawn in the rubbing process.

The final effect depends entirely on good composition. It is essential that the symbols should have clear forms which do not conflict with one another too strongly. The background spaces must also be well related in size, position and form, not only to one another but also to the symbols themselves.

J 15 ### Texture of Lines, Constructively related (17 upwards)

> Measured drawing. Drawing block, pencil or ballpoint pen, T-square or set-square, pair of compasses.

Abstract play with compasses and ruler is today considered a legitimate part of art education. There is a continuous line of development from the child's experiments with compasses to tangential constructions of the highest mathematical curves. The beauty of such constructions delight the receptive eye and stimulates the development of artistic sensibility (Plate 23 a).

Method

We place two straight lines at an angle and punctuate them at regular intervals with little dots. If these dots are joined to one another in turn by lines crossing one another, a curve results like a parabola produced by tangential construction. The idea of our exercise is based on this initial system which may consist of curved basic co-ordinates (e.g. a circle). The initial system is always to some extent veiled, so that the textures of tangents may achieve their full effect and through them the mysteriously resulting curves. An almost unlimited number of initial systems and a corresponding number of resulting curve rhythms are possible. Circle within circle, with varying numbers of points of co-ordination, produce spiral curves if the points are all co-ordinated in the same direction of revolution (e.g. all clockwise). An initial system of two intersecting circles with

182

an equal number of points of co-ordination produces ellipses. Hyperbola-shaped curves can also be produced if the initial system is two intersecting straight lines, and so on. Another method of procedure is in principle equally justified: one in which the resulting curves, the envisaged constituents of the picture, are anticipated and the tangents constituting the curves carefully added afterwards as effective linear textures, without the use of any initial system. Our main concern is not with construction itself but with visual experience.

Further themes: Solid Blocks flexibly related; Blown Blots of Colour; Transparent Intersection of Upright and Horizontal Coloured Rectangles; Chaos Resolving Itself; Musical Rhythms; Sacrament; Continuous-Line Drawing in Right Angles; Parallel Arrangement of Obtuse Angles; Ink Symbols with Blurred Outlines on a Wet Ground; Joy.

VI CONSTRUCTIONAL THEMES

GROUND-PLANS AND ELEVATIONS

K 1 **My Ideal Room: Ground-Plan and Arrangement of Furniture (13 upwards)**

> Drawing block, ruler, pencil, scissors, perhaps coloured paper, glue.

Almost all schoolchildren long to design the room of their own dreams, to be able to make the kind of furniture they want and to arrange it in their own way. This can be done at least theoretically for through the imagination everything we desire is within our reach.

Method

We start by deciding the proportions of the ground-plan and the positions of windows and doors. What proportion of length to breadth is ideal? How many extra square feet of living space would be afforded by a bay frontage? What should be the measurements of the large swivel window? For the dream furniture, movable plans are cut out of coloured paper and then everyone begins a kind of jigsaw game, trying all the possible arrangements of the room. What an enormous number there are; which is the most effective and original? When at length a satisfactory solution is found, the furniture is gummed in place.

K 2 **Design for a House (14 upwards)**

> Drawing block, ruler, pencil, perhaps drawing nib and penholder and ink, compasses.

We decide on a scale of 1:100 or 1:200, according to the size of our drawing paper. We next consider the number of rooms our particular family will need, and the proportionate size, the function and degree of importance of each room. Then we can start the designing of the layout of all the rooms within the dwelling complex.

Method

(Pupils to whom this procedure is entirely new may be helped by playing a ground-plan layout game, as under K1, except that this time the rooms themselves are being moved.)

184

What a variety of factors have to be taken into account! The function of individual rooms in the life of the family must be clearly reflected in the ground-plan (Plate 23 b). The kitchen must be next to the dining-room, which may be a part of the living-room. Bathroom, W.C. and cloakroom should form an independent subordinate complex and be near the entrance. A porch is useful at all seasons. As many rooms as possible should have direct access to the central hall. Some of them may be communicating, others separate. It would be better for the bedrooms to face east, the living-rooms south and west and the kitchen north, if this is practicable. Good window lighting is essential as dark corners are a disadvantage. Part of the architect's art consists in making the best possible use of the space at his disposal. We learn much from considering all these questions. A visit to a well-planned house and the study of some contemporary designs would also be instructive. What teaches us most, however, is our own naive attempt to tackle the problem constructively, which alone enables us fully to appreciate the work of great designers.

Elevations for this exercise will normally be for the exterior of the house. The architectural design of the exterior must inevitably depend upon the ground-plan but presents its own problems which have to be tackled afresh, in spite of the remaining link with the ground-plan.

Design for a Church (15 upwards) K 3

Drawing block, compasses and ruler, drawing pen, waterproof ink.

In the art-lesson each of us gets the chance to be a church architect just for once and to design a new and beautiful 'house of God'. For whoever has taken such a task upon himself and tried to carry it out as well as he can, will have eyes to recognise an architectural masterpiece and standards by which to judge and value it.

Method

Obviously a schoolchild approaches such a task naively, without any clear conception either of the long history or of the modern problems of church architecture. This ignorance has its pitfalls but also its advantages. Art-teaching must, above all, allow youthful optimism the freedom to enjoy its first experimental contact with the environment and its attempt actively to influence that environment. We can confidently assume the existence of this boundless self-confidence in children whose innately constructive fantasy has found expression in the familiar church theme, in spontaneous play with building blocks. We therefore impose no restrictive traditional demands, either theological, liturgical or purely architectural, no static or physical frontiers, for this is still 'play within the sanctuary of the ideal'. The young have confidence in their powers as long as no external law is imposed. Let us have confidence in our own teaching experience which has shown a thousand times that such freedom allows beauty to grow out of youthful longing for self-realisation.

Further themes: Ground-plan of our Classroom: Architectural Survey; Elevation of our School: Architectural Survey; Furniture and Equipment of a Flat: Placing Game; A New School Building; Youth Hostel; Indoor Swimming-Pool; Exhibition Hall; Ground-plan of St Paul's Cathedral; Front Elevation of a Cathedral; Plan of a Town.

DIAGRAMMATIC DESIGNS

K 4　My Dream House (16 upwards)

> Drawing block, pencil, ballpoint pen or drawing pen and ink.

The constructive imagination of many children is frustrated. The often promising early period of building play of a small child almost invariably ends abruptly when he starts school. Our city-bred children often sadly miss the opportunities for wider practical creation which would have been all around them in a natural environment. Schools have hitherto done little to supply this need. The art-class is the right psychological moment to release the choked-up springs of creative energy.

　For adolescents, the making of diagrammatic designs provides encouragement and preparation for a new serious building play (see model buildings under K 13-15). Diagrammatic designs are intended to be free drawings of architectural ideas unimpeded by considerations of perspective accuracy.

Method

The kind of diagrammatic designs we have in mind need not be realisable either in the static architectonic or in the practical functional sense. Ground-plan and elevation are one way of expressing architectural ideas. The diagrammatic drawing aims beyond these abstract schemata at bringing the solid building before our eyes. It aims to show the building as fully and simultaneously as possible. It therefore shows at least two sides of the solid form. In other words it visualises and represents from a diagonal viewpoint, from above.

Children's very early drawings already show more than one side of a house at a time. The diagrammatic drawing is thus a natural development of the fundamental idea of drawing. Its technique is developed intuitively. Therefore the only restriction which the teacher imposes is the rule which applies to all drawing, namely that pretence and confusion must be avoided.

The High-Diving Tower (15 upwards) K 5

Drawing block, pencil, black ballpoint pen or drawing pen and ink.

As we are keenly interested in sport, we might design a high-diving tower for our open-air swimming-pool. The point of departure of the exercise is therefore a purely practical consideration. We have to discuss the number, height and relative positions of the diving boards and platforms and what design would be realisable in practice. At the same time we shall not be content to produce a merely functional structure. To fulfil our artistic purpose it must be shapely as well as functional in design.

Method

Many modern swimming-pools possess high-diving towers of great architectural beauty. Moreover, they are often miracles of engineering. When we consider the thousands to whom these strange giant water-plants have become familiar sights, we cannot help asking ourselves how many of these people ever look at what was after all intended to delight the eye as much as for any other purpose.

A personal attempt to create a form is the best means of developing appreciation of the created forms which surround us. One must first experience for oneself how difficult it is to give a noble form to something which has to fulfil a definite practical function, before one can recognise the mind of a great artist in the design of an apparently simple form.

187

Design of Stage Scenery (16 upwards)

Tinted Drawing. Drawing block, pencil, colour box and brush.

The theme of stage scenery is exactly suited to a diagrammatic design. Since all theatrical objects are pretences, everything is allowable, even the most 'unreal' combination and construction. The design of stage décor is thus one of the freest forms of art; although it fulfils a certain function, the fantastic whims of the artist are allowed full scope. Such freedom always furthers art education.

Method

It is advisable to choose a play or opera that the children know and which is well within their grasp. This can best be done in co-operation with the literature or drama teacher. Without forestalling the independent ideas of the designers, we may follow the author's stage directions as to the essential attributes of the scene. Each individual is free to interpret them according to his creative ability. It is possible to conform to the author's requirements in every detail and yet to create innumerable entirely different sets. The author's description of the scene has then the same relation to its individual interpretations as a picture dictation (see H 1-15) to the resulting pictures.

Further themes: Multi-story Car-park; Theatre Building; Memorial Building; Studio Building; Garden Café; Concert Pavilion; Kiosk; Writing Desk; Bookcase.

ISOMETRIC CONSTRUCTION

K 7 **Factory Plant (14 upwards)**

Measured drawing (see *150 Techniques in Art,* p. 77). Drawing block, or drawing board and paper, pencil, compasses, ruler, set-square.

Isometric drawing is so-called because a three-dimensional representation of solid objects is made on the plane of the paper, in such a way that the length and breadth of the ground-plan and elevations remain unforeshortened. (Isometry means retention of equal measurements.) The angles of the ground-plan are also unchanged. This is made possible by turning the ground-plan, which appears in its original shape, by an angle to the picture edge and using it as the basic determinent of the ensuing structure of parallels. The unshortened lines of elevation are then based on the corners of the ground-plan and a three-dimensional drawing is thus produced.

Method

A factory plant may consist of various rectangular flat-roofed buildings of different heights, with a few tall, wide chimneys. The parallel lines of the ground-plan are laid at an angle to the edge of the picture but without modification of angles or fore-shortening of lines. Upon the angles of this ground-plan we base the lines of elevation, also unchanged, and join them to the roof. The chimneys become narrower towards their tops; we base their elevation on the exact centre of a circle and this gives us the centre of a smaller circle for the top of the chimney. Further helps to construction can easily be evolved in the course of the work. At the end, the lines of construction and lines which would be invisible in a solid object are rubbed out.

Half-timbered Building under Construction (15 upwards)   K 8

> Measured drawing. Drawing block, pencil, compasses, ruler, set-square, drawing pen or penholder and drawing nib, ink or designer's colour.

One can start building the little house on squared, timber corner-pillars, just as one would base four round pillars of equal height on four small circles at the corners of a rectangle to build an outdoor extension roof for clothes-drying. This method of building up from the ground, floor by floor, is the basis of our theme.

Method

An isometric representation of a building shows a parallel per-spective in which there is no foreshortening of lines or dis-tortion of angles of horizontal planes (see K 7 and *150 Techniques in Art*, p. 77). Thus the squared timbers of the corner-posts retain the same square cross-section at all levels. We can add further uprights to constitute the walls of the house and to raise the triangular, gabled front, and also further horizontal, squared timbers to complete all the timbered framework of the building. The resulting divisions can be bricked up, used for

189

door and window spaces and partly left empty. By joining the apex of the gable to the corners of the house, we obtain the sloping roof and in like manner the ridge of the roof. The roof is then close-timbered with lighter lathes to support the slates. On the roof too we shall reveal the process of building by leaving part of the timbers uncovered.

K 9   Cathedral (16 upwards)

Isometric drawing (see *150 Techniques in Art,* p. 77). Drawing block or drawing board and paper, pencil, compasses, ruler, set-square, drawing pen or penholder and drawing nib, ink or designer's colour.

Isometric drawings of Romanesque and Gothic cathedrals are rewarding exercises for the seniors. My pupils of the Upper Sixth drew 25 of the beautiful churches in their city in this way. The initial problem was the drawing of the ground-plan and elevations. We found much of the necessary information in books and the rest by walking about and surveying the buildings themselves.

Method

The ground-plan of a Romanesque cathedral may be divided into several parts (nave, side aisles, transept, choir and apse), distinct yet fused together like crystals. We lay the ground-plan, unforeshortened, at an angle of 30 or 60 degrees to the edge of the paper, in the lower part of the picture area. Each part of the building is then separately constructed from its own position; the unshortened measurements of the lines of elevation are always maintained (Plate 22 c). Not until all the parts of the building are united and all superfluous lines of construction have been rubbed out, can detail such as windows, frieze, blind arcades, niches, and mouldings be added. The construction of the roof and tower presents the most difficulty, but pupils will be able to understand how to do it after some simple explanation.

Further themes: Standard Lamp; A Miniature Town; A Workroom; Spiral Staircase; A Summer-house; A Gymnasium; Modern Housing Estate; Skyscraper; A Building Constructed from Building Blocks; A Fair or Exhibition Hall.

Surrealist Room (17 upwards) K 10

> Central-point perspective. Drawing block, ruler and compasses, pencil, box of poster colours, brush.

The simple rules of the central-point method can be used as the conventions of the game for many constructional pictures. The intersection of the two diagonals of the drawing paper gives us our central point at which all receding lines (horizontal parallels) meet. Thus, according to the central perspective convention, the central point serves as the only vanishing point within the picture. The remaining horizontals on the picture plane run parallel to the ground-plane of picture, the remaining perpendicular lines at right angles to it.

Method

The four sectors of the picture plane produced by the diagonals are to be considered as the enclosing planes of an endlessly receding space, which begins on the whole picture plane and may be closed by a smaller rectangle in the centre of the picture. This would produce an empty 'room'. The rules of our game allow us to give this room doors, windows, a tiled floor, etc., and to fill it with cubic structures as its surrealistic 'furniture'. Into this strange room we introduce an equally strange puppet-like figure whose gestures are abstract (Plate 23 c).

Probably, in the course of paving the floor with chess-board tiles, the pupils will discover that the rows must be foreshortened more and more the further one goes into the room. Simple aids to construction can solve this problem, though the measuring-point method already suggests itself. This method however scarcely belongs to our school drawing course. Pupils with a mathematical bent may be shown that the method is based on the angle of vision but, in general, it is advisable to adapt the solutions of this problem to the needs and interest of the particular class.

Dwelling in the Year 3000 (15 upwards) K 11

> Measured drawing. Drawing block, pencil, ruler, penholder and drawing nib, ink or designer's colour.

If we compare one of the great dwelling 'hives' of a modern city with a Victorian house, we can measure the change a century has brought. The distance between the two periods, both in the spiritual and the physical sense, is greater than that between the Victorians and the ancient Greeks. It is impossible to imagine the distant future of this line of development. Writers, however, have for some time occupied themselves to a much greater extent than architects with futuristic fantasies, and many of their prophecies have been fulfilled.

Method

The English composition and the art class are the occasions when the Utopian fantasies of schoolchildren can come into their own. What will a house look like in the year 3000? What young brain is not stimulated by such a question to dream daring dreams? No boundaries are set. Anything is possible. All the same we shall make the proviso—or the suggestion— that the building should have a basically constructivist character on purely artistic grounds, lest foam-rubber or mud-pie architecture should result. Our Utopian architectural designs are not intended arrogantly to deny artistic ability to our descendants by ascribing formless design to the architects of the future.

K 12 A Picture by a Constructivist Painter (16 upwards)

> Painting in poster or powder colours. Drawing block or other painting surface, box of poster colours or powder colours with size, pencil and ruler, sable or bristle brush.

The constructivist school of painting was influenced to a considerable extent by the Bauhaus school, although it was a phenomenon of the 1920s and was already in the air somewhat earlier. Its most distinguished representatives, among whom were Mondrian and Moholy-Nagy, made decisive contributions to the art of the twentieth century, the influence of which is still active today. As a territory of exploration Constructivism still has great potentialities, although its extreme heights have already been scaled. The abstract dream of a marriage between geometry and art still inspires contemporary painters to considerable work.

Method

Senior pupils are well able to express the influence of constructivist art in their own work. That is why I now set them the task of, so to speak, impersonating a constructivist painter at work, or rather of inventing the work of an imaginary constructivist just as a novelist invents his characters and their deeds. Experience of the psychological development of the young shows that such a task is admirably suited to adolescents. Its abstract form makes no objective demands and concentrates the attention entirely upon the creation of a perfect balance of forms and colour. It therefore appears easy to the pupil. Through direct experience of this style of art, he will come to realise that great variation of artistic ability can be manifest in it.

Further themes: Skeleton of a Fantastic Tower; City in Space; Surrealist Architectonic Design; Constructivist Study of Water Patterns; Tectonic Landscape; Surrealist Furniture; Constructivist Drawing of a Head; Constructivist Still-Life; Exhibition of Constructivist Paintings and Sculpture; Constructivist Poster.

MODELS

Romanesque Church (13 upwards)   K 13

Architectural model (see *150 Techniques in Art,* p. 78-9). One-mm bookbinding board or stiff cardboard (posterboard or folder cover) ruler, compasses, pencil, scissors, if necessary bookbinding knife, gummed paper strips, powder colours with size base.

As in the isometric drawing of architecture (see K 7-9), we first need to decide the measurements (reduced to scale) of the ground-plan and elevations. We get them either from a pamphlet or by measuring or assessing the measurements of the original, or from a good photograph.

Method

The method of modelling we are going to adopt is to analyse and separate the various parts of the building and to construct them separately before combining them to form the whole model. Here is an example: a small Romanesque church consists of about four distinct parts, the nave ending with the rounded wall of the chancel, the short north and south arms of the transept, and a square tower. These four parts can be 'dismantled' and drawn in the flat on the cardboard, cut out, and shaped again separately. Finally the four parts can easily

193

be assembled and stuck together with glue and gummed tape (for strengthening the corners and seams).

It is best to give the bare cardboard model one or several coats of thick powder colour which will hide any visible joins. Architectural detail, such as windows, friezes, and doors, can be painted with poster colours.

K 14 A Painter's House (15 upwards)

> Cardboard model (see *150 Techniques in Art,* pp. 78-9). One-mm *Passe-partout* board or folder cover board, pencil, compasses, ruler, scissors, gummed paper strips, strong cardboard base.

Building a scale-model of an ideal house for a painter involves designing the ground-plan and elevations on which the measurements of our three-dimensional representation must be based.

Method

We start the model by carefully transferring the measurements of all the planes of the building to the cardboard with ruler and compasses. Adjoining planes are drawn spread out adjacent to one another on the flat surface, like the parts of an outspread garment. Flaps for joining are needed only if no gummed paper is available, so that liquid glue has to be used. When the flat area has been cut out, the corners to be bent are lightly scored with a sharp knife against a ruler. The subordinate projecting parts of the building are best set up separately and joined to the main building afterwards. The completed model is glued to a firm cardboard or plywood base (Plate 24b). The flat surfaces of large or small windows, of doors and of the roof, may be represented by pieces of coloured paper pasted into position.

K 15 Large Filling Station (15 upwards)

> Cardboard model (see *150 Techniques in Art,* pp. 78-9). One-mm *Passe-partout* board, pencil, compasses, ruler, scissors, gummed paper strips, adhesive, strong board as a base.

There is one field of functional architectonic design which allows more scope to the imagination than others. In the design of all those buildings which are intended mainly to attract attention or to advertise, such as fair and exhibition halls, kiosks and petrol stations, imaginative form and free play with building materials and techniques are not merely permissible but indispensable.

Method

When, after all kinds of experiment, an idea has taken shape and been carried as far as the drawings of the plan view and elevations to a suitable scale (1:20), the model can be built up from its foundations like a real building. The 'ground' is first measured out as the ground-plan is transferred to the carboard base. The building itself develops rather like a prefabricated house, since walls and roofs are made at the same time in one flat piece (see K 13 and 14). Here too the more complex and multiform parts of the building are assembled from their separately made parts. Only accurate, tidy workmanship will produce a successful model. Therein lies the educational value of the exercise, which leads from free imagination into craftsmanship and aims to develop the habit of conscientious and concentrated work.

Further themes: Model of a Stage; Model of a Living-room; Suspension Bridge; Staircase; Utopian Buildings; Skyscraper; Exhibition Building; Youth Hostel; Model of a Church; Open-air-Swimming-pool.

Index of Techniques

The majority of the themes described are intended for
Painting in Poster or Powder Colours.
The following techniques are also used: